Purchased for Library Buildings
April 2004
Dalston

# INFORMATION POWER

Guidelines for
School Library
Media Programs

D0879248

# *INFORMATION POWER*

## Guidelines for School Library Media Programs

Prepared by the AMERICAN ASSOCIATION OF SCHOOL LIBRARIANS and ASSOCIATION FOR EDUCATIONAL COMMUNICATIONS AND TECHNOLOGY

AMERICAN LIBRARY ASSOCIATION
*Chicago and London*
and
ASSOCIATION FOR EDUCATIONAL COMMUNICATIONS
AND TECHNOLOGY
*Washington, D.C.*

This publication can be purchased from the
AMERICAN LIBRARY ASSOCIATION
50 East Huron Street, Chicago, Illinois 60611
or from the
ASSOCIATION FOR EDUCATIONAL COMMUNICATIONS
AND TECHNOLOGY
1126 Sixteenth Street, NW, Washington, D.C. 20036

**Library of Congress Cataloging-in-Publication Data**

American Association of School Librarians and Association
    for Educational Communications and Technology.
    Information power.

    Bibliography: p.
    Includes index.
    1. School libraries—Standards.  2. Media programs
(Education)—Standards.  I. American Association
of School Librarians.  II. Association for Educational
Communications and Technology.  III. Title.
Z675.S3S743  1988          027.8            88-3480
ISBN 0-8389-3352-1

Copyright ©1988 by the American Library Association and the Association for
Educational Communications and Technology. All rights reserved except those
which may be granted by Sections 107 and 108 of the Copyright Revision Act of
1976.

Printed in the United States of America.
96        11 10 9

# Contents

# Preface

Professional standards have always been a dynamic, positive force for change. Such documents have provided the philosophical framework from which school library media programs have evolved. Standards have often shifted the direction of the profession.

The first standards for secondary school libraries were prepared by the Committee on Library Organization and Equipment of the National Educational Association (NEA) and published by the American Library Association (ALA) in 1920. This document established standards for senior high schools of varying sizes and junior high schools. The report was followed by *Elementary School Library Standards,* prepared by a joint committee of the NEA and ALA, and published by ALA in 1925. ALA published the first set of national K–12 school library standards, *School Libraries for Today and Tomorrow,* in 1945. These postwar standards formed the historical precedent for today's school library media programs. These early standards differentiated between the role of the school librarian and the public librarian. They also defined the service functions that the building-level library and the public library provided to schools.

In 1960, American Association of School Librarians (AASL) prepared *Standards for School Library Programs* that were published by ALA. These standards addressed changes that had occurred in the school library media program between 1945 and 1960. In this document, the role of the school librarian changed significantly, with a major emphasis placed on serving students and teachers. Services offered directly to students were given priority and centered on enriching their personal and instructional activities. The scope of the school library program was expanded to include audiovisual materials; standards were identified for audiovisual materials and services. *Standards for School Library Programs* emphasized that good school library programs made audiovisual materials easily accessible. The document urged school librarians to work closely with teachers in the selection and use of all types of media materials. The 1960 standards also emphasized the role of the school librarian as a teacher. In this role, the school librarian was jointly responsible with the classroom teacher for teaching library skills as an integrated part of the classroom instruction.

In the mid 1960s, financial support for upgrading and expanding public education and school programs increased significantly. School library programs benefited greatly from the infusion of new resources. Also during this time, great numbers of professional personnel entered the field. As a result of this growth, AASL and the Department of Audiovisual Instruction of the National Educational Association (DAVI, now AECT), in cooperation with several other national associations, prepared *Standards for School Media Programs,* published in 1969. The name of these standards and the joint authorship emphasized the changing role of the school library program. All media, print and nonprint, were recognized as equally important. New terms such as *media, media specialist, media center,* and *media program* were used to show the broad focus and scope of the unified program. Staffing patterns focused on specialization of professional and paraprofessional positions in order to meet the needs of the unified media program. The document further reinforced the scope of the media program by emphasizing unified certification requirements encompassing both the school library and audiovisual areas.

The 1969 standards also emphasized the changing role of the school media specialist in working with teacher and students. School media specialists were expected to work with classroom teachers in the analysis of instructional needs, the design of learning activities using existing and new technologies, and the production of needed materials to support the classroom curriculum. The 1969 standards also stressed the role of the media specialist in helping students develop competence in listening, viewing, and reading skills.

In 1975, AASL and AECT collaborated on *Media Programs:*

*District and School* as a result of the continuing development of the role of the library media specialist. These standards reflected the influence of a systems approach to media services. Programs designed to respond to both district and school objectives were described. The 1975 publication advocated the importance of the planning process to determine the needs of individual media programs. By providing sets of "guiding principles" to aid in local program decisions, *Media Programs: District and School* served as guidelines as well as standards. Unlike previous standards, this document addressed the importance of the media program at the district level in support of the building-level media program. *Media Programs* stressed the library media specialist's involvement with classroom teachers in the instructional design process. Through these standards, the role of the media program changed from a support service to an integral part of the total instructional program of the school.

As a result of significant changes within education during the past decade and of the effect of expanded access to new sources of information, AASL and AECT developed INFORMATION POWER: GUIDELINES FOR SCHOOL LIBRARY MEDIA PROGRAMS. This document extends the concept begun in *Media Programs: District and School* of aiding local professionals in decision-making; it provides the vision and guidance necessary for the school library media program to significantly expand the access to and use of information and ideas by students, teachers, and parents.

# Introduction

INFORMATION POWER: GUIDELINES FOR SCHOOL LIBRARY ME-
DIA PROGRAMS sets forth guidelines for developing the school li-
brary media programs needed to prepare students for personal
success in the next century. Developed jointly by the American
Association of School Librarians (AASL) and the Association for
Educational Communications and Technology (AECT), INFORMA-
TION POWER replaces *Media Programs: District and School* pub-
lished in 1975.

During the past decade, the proliferation of information resources and the development of new technologies have broadened
and redefined the mission of the school library media program
and the role of the library media specialist. AASL and AECT have
worked together to prepare new guidelines that provide a sound
philosophical basis for the continued development of school library media programs to meet the needs of students in the twenty-
first century.

The project began in the spring of 1983, when appointments
to the Standards Writing Committee were jointly made by AASL
and AECT. After two years of work, the original committee was reorganized into a four-member writing team and a reactor panel.
The writing team submitted the first draft of the guidelines document in April 1987. Two additional drafts, each reviewed by national leaders, were completed before an open forum was held in
conjunction with the AECT Leadership Conference in early Au-
gust 1987. Affiliate officers in each state had the opportunity to review drafts during the entire process, and some held special
meetings to solicit comments from their members. Following additional review and subsequent revision during the fall of 1987, the

document was approved by the AASL and the AECT boards in January 1988.

The primary focus of these guidelines is the building-level library media specialist. Library media specialists are responsible for the design and delivery of effective library media programs. These guidelines emphasize a planning philosophy, stressing that the specific and unique needs of the school curriculum determine the type and level of program offered. INFORMATION POWER is based on the premise that teachers, principals, and library media specialists must form a partnership and plan together to design and implement the program that best matches the instructional needs of the school.

The document also emphasizes the building-level school library media specialist's responsibility to exercise leadership in establishing the partnerships and initiating the planning process. This leadership is essential if the vision of the school library media program depicted in INFORMATION POWER is to be realized.

Promoting effective physical access to information resources and intellectual access to the content is the central unifying concept of these guidelines. Library media specialists serve as the link between students, teachers, administrators, and parents and the available information resources. The roles and services defined in this document are dynamic; they are changing and evolving in response to the societal, economic, and technological demands on education.

Quantitative recommendations are made only when professional consensus and research provide a solid basis of support, such as in the areas of personnel and facilities. The document does, however, include quantitative information on school library media programs, based upon research conducted by the U.S. Department of Education, as guidance for planning and evaluating new and existing programs. While quantitative data in previous documents reflected the best professional judgment at the time, the quantitative data in Appendix A reflect existing conditions in high school services programs during the 1984–85 school year. The data are not included as recommendations but rather as illustrations of the varying levels of support provided for library media programs at that time.

AASL, AECT, and the entire school library media profession owe a debt of gratitude to the many contributors who donated personal time to this effort. In addition, many state associations and individuals, as well as ALA Publishing Services, donated funds for the writing project. Special thanks go to the members of the Writing Team, the Writing Committee, and the special consultants who shaped the philosophy upon which the document is based. Members of both boards and many leaders of both AASL and AECT devoted numerous hours reviewing and refining the document throughout its development. A listing of key contributors may be found in Appendix F.

INFORMATION POWER: GUIDELINES FOR SCHOOL LIBRARY MEDIA PROGRAMS provides a vision for developing and implementing quality programs. We challenge you to use it to empower the students and faculty in your school through the resources and services of your school library media program.

KAREN A. WHITNEY, AASL President
ELAINE K. DIDIER, AECT President

# The Mission and the Challenges

## The Mission

**The mission of the library media program is to ensure that students and staff are effective users of ideas and information.** This mission is accomplished:

- by providing intellectual and physical access to materials in all formats
- by providing instruction to foster competence and stimulate interest in reading, viewing, and using information and ideas
- by working with other educators to design learning strategies to meet the needs of individual students.

The mission of the school library media program encompasses a number of specific objectives:

1. **to provide intellectual access to information** through systematic learning activities which develop cognitive strategies for selecting, retrieving, analyzing, evaluating, synthesizing, and creating information at all age levels and in all curriculum content areas
2. **to provide physical access to information** through (a) a carefully selected and systematically organized collection of diverse learning resources, representing a wide range of subjects, levels of difficulty, communication formats, and technological delivery systems; (b) access to information and materials outside the library media center and the school building through such mechanisms as interlibrary loan, networking and other cooperative agreements, and online searching of databases; and (c) provid-

ing instruction in the operation of equipment necessary to use the information in any format

3. **to provide learning experiences that encourage users to become discriminating consumers and skilled creators of information** through introduction to the full range of communications media and use of the new and emerging information technologies

4. **to provide leadership, instruction, and consulting assistance in the use of instructional and information technology** and the use of sound instructional design principles

5. **to provide resources and activities that contribute to lifelong learning**, while accommodating a wide range of differences in teaching and learning styles and in instructional methods, interests, and capacities

6. **to provide a facility that functions as the information center of the school**, as a locus for integrated, interdisciplinary, intergrade, and school-wide learning activities

7. **to provide resources and learning activities** that represent a diversity of experiences, opinions, social and cultural perspectives, supporting the concept that intellectual freedom and access to information are prerequisite to effective and responsible citizenship in a democracy.

It is the responsibility of the school library media specialist and the district library media director to take the lead in translating the mission into programs that make effective access to information and ideas a reality. However, achievement of this mission at both school and district levels also requires:

full integration of the library media program into the curriculum

a partnership among the library media specialist, district-level personnel, administrators, teachers, and parents

the serious commitment of each of those partners to the value of universal and unrestricted access to information and ideas.

## The Challenges

A number of challenges face school library media specialists as they seek to fulfill the mission of the program. The challenges result from a variety of influences and have the potential to radically reshape the services school library media specialists offer, the environment in which they work, and the profession to which they belong. To determine the implications of those challenges for library media programs, it is important to examine briefly some of the influences that produced them.

CHALLENGE 1:    To provide intellectual and physical access to information and ideas for a diverse population whose needs are changing rapidly

### The Context

Change—rapid and pervasive—may be the single most important characteristic of life in the twentieth century. Social and technological change is occurring at such a rate that techniques for managing it often seem outdated before they can be properly implemented. There is a profound preoccupation with the future and with the unpredictable consequences of change.

American society is becoming more and more diverse, both culturally and linguistically, as minority ethnic groups begin to constitute larger proportions of the total population. Further, the traditional pattern of assimilation of immigrant groups into the American cultural mainstream has changed. Cultural diversity is now widely perceived as desirable, and present-day ethnic groups are preserving their ethnic identity.

Other major changes in the social and economic makeup of society have occurred over the last two decades. There are more women in the work force, and so there are more families in which all the adults work outside the home. More children live with one parent—a fact which economists and sociologists cite as bearing on the increase in the number of children who live in poverty. Families break up and re-form into new families. The population of many communities is less stable because Americans move more often—once every six years on the average, according to the Census Bureau's latest study of geographical mobility.

Further, with the increased interdependence of the world's economies, events in parts of the world that once seemed distant visibly affect America's social and economic fabric. Telecommunications enhance that visibility, giving to distant events the immediacy of happenings in our own neighborhood or community. Within this volatile environment, schools are responsible for educating students who will spend most of their lives in the twenty-first century.

There is an emerging consensus that, if children are to be prepared for a future characterized by change, they must learn to think rationally and creatively, to solve problems, to manage and retrieve information, and to communicate effectively. As a consequence, current and future curriculum development at all grade levels will stress the teaching of core competencies and skills, which are transferable across disciplines, applicable to any learning situation, regardless of content.

Basic to the achievement of these objectives are the skills needed to fully use the potential of the information world throughout life. The individual who reaches adulthood without these skills will find it difficult to adapt well to changing circumstances.

### Implications

Library media specialists are concerned about meeting the changing and complex needs of students, teachers, and others they serve, and they must consider the following important questions:

- How does the library media specialist serve so many diverse populations with complex needs?
- How does the library media specialist help students to acquire the skills, knowledge, and attitudes needed to function effectively in the twenty-first century?
- What is the library media specialist's responsibility in working with administrators and teachers to plan and implement an integrated curriculum focusing on interdisciplinary higher-order thinking skills?
- How does the library media specialist effectively promote new and existing information and instructional resources and technologies and ensure that they are used effectively by teachers to prepare students to flourish in a dramatically changing world?

**CHALLENGE 2:**   To ensure equity and freedom of access to information and ideas, unimpeded by social, cultural, economic, geographic, or technologic constraints

### The Context

School library media programs have traditionally provided the school community with print and nonprint resources. In doing so, school library media specialists have always had to cope with a variety of access issues, among them: physical access for the handicapped, access for children confined to their homes, censorship, and copyright.

Censorship efforts flourish in this time, as they always have. Some individuals and organized groups believe that schools should be purged of books, materials, and courses that contain ideas that conflict with their own convictions. The library media specialist must continue to maintain free access to materials through collection development policies, as well as program and access policies.

Issues resulting from the fair use of copyrighted materials continue to affect the school library media program. While the fair use guidelines for print materials are well defined and supported by case law, fair use guidelines for audiovisual and computer resources are not as clearly delineated. The issue of the fair use of many materials is further complicated by readily available and inexpensive duplication techniques. In all cases, library media specialists must adhere to and promote the legal and ethical use of copyrighted materials. The protection and recognition of the rights of the copyright holder will ensure continued development of quality instructional materials.

While such issues continue to affect freedom of access, we are in the midst of a communications revolution that poses new challenges. When first introduced, new technologies are frequently expensive and sometimes complex to operate. Students who are not adequately trained in their use or who are without sufficient financial resources are effectively denied access.

Technology also poses important ethical issues regarding access to information, raising questions about student and staff rights and responsibilities in the areas of information security and privacy. When technology is used more frequently to monitor student work, control circulation, or find information in national databases, records are amassed that have the potential to violate a student's or a teacher's right to privacy.

### Implications

Access to the free flow of useful knowledge and information is essential to the individual's ability to thrive in a world characterized by complex information systems. Library media specialists are dedicated to providing access to information and ideas for all those served by the library media program, and they must consider the following important questions:

- How does the library media specialist provide the resources and services that create and sustain an atmosphere of free inquiry and guarantee students access to a broad range of ideas and information?
- How can the resources be obtained to offer the existing and emerging information technologies in sufficient quantities to meet the needs of all users?
- How does the library media specialist ensure student and staff rights to privacy?

- What is the responsibility of the library media specialist in developing school district policies and procedures to deal with copyright issues?
- What is the responsibility of the school library media specialist for ensuring that students and faculty have the skills needed to use the new and emerging technologies?

CHALLENGE 3: To promote literacy and the enjoyment of reading, viewing, and listening for young people at all ages and stages of development

### The Context

The major school reform efforts undertaken during the 1980s have placed strong emphasis on the improvement of reading comprehension skills, which support learning in the content area. According to the National Assessment of Educational Progress report, *Learning to Be Literate in America,* nearly 50 percent of young adults tested were unable to demonstrate the advanced reading comprehension skills of analysis and synthesis.

Healthy debate continues about the relative merits of different methods of teaching literacy competencies to diverse student populations. Basal reading series and kits of programmed materials are the rule in some classrooms, while in others a mix of trade, text, and locally produced materials may be found. Many of the newer reading programs draw on an established body of children's and adolescent literature for their reading selections and associated activities, and incorporate reading with other language arts: listening, speaking, and writing.

*Becoming a Nation of Readers,* the landmark report issued by the National Academy of Education's Commission on Reading, makes strong recommendations for improving reading and language comprehension, emphasizes the importance of student motivation, imaginative, and flexible teaching, and encourages home and school environments that stimulate and support literacy. The report stresses independent reading of literature and information books, as well as careful selection and judicious use of textbooks, and recommends that "Schools should maintain well-stocked and managed libraries...[and] a librarian who encourages wide reading and helps match books to children." The library media program is seen as vital for motivating young people

to select and read printed materials with pleasure, to reach for more complex levels of expression and comprehension, and to evaluate these experiences critically.

The importance of libraries was again emphasized in *What Works: Research about Teaching and Learning,* second edition, published by the U.S. Department of Education in 1987; "Public and school libraries can enhance reading instruction by offering literature-based activities that stress the enjoyment of reading as well as reading skills. . . . Use of both public and school libraries encourages students to go beyond their textbooks to locate, explore, evaluate and use ideas and information that enhance classroom instruction."

### Implications

Current trends in reading instruction reinforce many of the traditional goals and objectives of school library media professionals: for example, more emphasis on comprehension skills and less on decoding skills; less dependency on textbook programs and more individualized reading and research in all the content areas; and the use of literature as integral to, rather than as enrichment of, the language arts program.

The importance of library media collections, programs, and specialists is being acknowledged in the efforts to improve education. Library media specialists must seize the opportunity offered by the renewed concern with literacy to exercise both leadership and support in their schools. In order to promote literacy and the enjoyment of reading, library media professionals must consider the following questions:

- What relationship should the library media specialist have with the reading specialist and the classroom teacher in regard to fostering literacy and reading comprehension in students?
- How does the library media specialist contribute to planning and implementing the language arts program? What is the decision-making process for choosing programs and materials, and who is involved?
- What special contributions do the library media specialist and program make to the student's development of advanced comprehension abilities?
- What special contributions do the library media specialist and program make to broadening the student's acquaintance and understanding of literature?
- How do the library media specialist and program foster in students the "library habit," and encourage independent reading for pleasure and information?

CHALLENGE 4:    To provide leadership and expertise in the use of information and instructional technologies

### The Context

Electronic print and image-based communication systems have had a profound impact on society. They make it possible to rapidly manipulate, store, transfer, and create information in many forms, and they have enormous potential for the development of new knowledge.

Miniaturization of equipment, expanded storage capacity, and reduced costs have led to the distribution of microcomputers in homes, schools, and offices. A steady increase in the creation and use of micro- and mainframe-based information systems is expected to continue. Online communication between users and large databases at remote sites is already well established. In the future, a growing number of these databases will be made available locally through advances in compact disc and fiber-optic technology.

Cable television, microwave relays, satellites, fiber-optics, and other broadcast technologies provide the means for making formal instruction and interpersonal communications readily accessible and increasingly inexpensive. Reduced costs of some technologies have already occurred, and other reductions are anticipated. Even more important than speed or cost are the broader learning options that these technologies make possible for the individual knowledge seeker and for groups working collaboratively.

### Implications

All aspects of education are significantly influenced by major technological advancements. The complexity of instructional technologies can, at times, overwhelm educators seeking ways to integrate them into the school curriculum. By assuming a leadership role in the use of technology in the school, the library media specialist promotes effective use of instructional technologies and facilitates their full integration into the curriculum.

The library media specialist provides expertise in evaluating, selecting, using, and managing the technologies that make information and ideas available in a wide variety of formats. As a leader in the school's technology planning process, the library

media specialist provides an assessment of the potential impact of various technologies and assists educators in making informed decisions about technologies appropriate to specific curriculum needs. Once a particular informational/instructional technology is adopted, the library media specialist assumes responsibility for educating faculty and students in its optimal use, either personally or by arranging for appropriate instruction.

To lead in this area, the library media specialist must possess the expertise necessary to evaluate, select, manage, and use existing and emerging technologies. The proliferation of information and technological advances demands that the library media specialist engage in continuing professional development.

Library media specialists are concerned with establishing and maintaining a leadership role in the uses of technology within the school and must consider the following important questions:

- How does the library media specialist obtain the initial knowledge and continuing professional development necessary to help students and teachers take full advantage of existing and emerging information and instructional technologies?
- How does the library media specialist help students learn to use all types of information systems effectively to make decisions, solve problems, and think creatively?

- How does the library media specialist promote new and existing information and instructional technologies and see that they are used effectively by teachers?
- How can the new technologies be used effectively to provide additional instructional and consulting time for the library media specialist to work with students and teachers?

### CHALLENGE 5:    To participate in networks that enhance access to resources located outside the school

#### The Context

Young people exhibit a vast range of natural interests and curiosities that are deepened and broadened by school assignments, class discussion, and interaction with teachers and peers. Teachers have an even greater range of information needs relating to their instructional responsibilities and professional development.

Few schools are equipped with the full variety of resources necessary to satisfy all of these needs, and many students and some teachers lack direct access to any other library or information agency. However, the library media program has the potential to provide effective access to numerous other agencies that can, as needed, supply vast amounts of the nation's total information resources.

Unfortunately, barriers to resource sharing may exist. Legal restrictions to lending or borrowing materials are sometimes invoked by school boards or municipal governments. The costs of networking—staff time, fees to participate, communication line charges, payments for catalogs and directories—can be substantial, even though state and federal governments sometimes subsidize their existence. Communication equipment is sometimes unequally distributed among school library media centers; some centers are equipped for online searching, while others are not equipped with a telephone. Often library media specialists do not have the planning time necessary to effectively participate in resource sharing.

#### Implications

The concept of structuring learning activities around the use of many and varied information sources is not new. It is, however, an approach to learning that is uniquely appropriate to the needs of today's learner. Library media specialists are concerned about creating partnerships that enhance access to resources located outside the school and must answer the following important questions:

- Which functions and services are best provided by local systems and by commercial vendors, and which are best provided by utilities and networks?
- How can traditional attitudinal and other barriers to resource sharing be overcome?
- How do library media programs fully and effectively participate in networks that meet the needs of members of the school community?
- How does the library media specialist use resource sharing to promote the concept of lifelong learning?
- How does the library media specialist promote partnerships with community agencies and businesses to broaden students' learning opportunities?

The school library media specialist will continue to be faced with complex challenges as expanding access to increasing amounts of information dictates the rethinking of traditional services and the provision of new services. Intelligent, careful planning is essential because programs rely on numerous discrete systems working in concert. Effective planning is the key to survival in an environment of accelerating change.

## Selected Readings

Haycock, Ken. "Strengthening the Foundations for Teacher-Librarianship." *School Library Media Quarterly* 13, no. 2 (Spring 1985): 102–109.

Keynote address to the 1984 conference of the International Association of School Librarianship in Honolulu, Hawaii. An important statement on the role and change of directions for the library media center.

Liesener, James W. "Learning at Risk: School Library Media Programs in an Information World." *School Library Media Quarterly* 13, no. 4 (Fall 1985): 11–20.

Presented for a series of seminars held January through March 1984, sponsored by the U.S. Department of Education, this was one of the papers in response to "A Nation At Risk."

*Chapter*

# The School Library Media Program

The school library media program encompasses all the resources and activities through which the library media staff translate the mission into reality. A variety of models exists for the
successful program. The activities and resources included in the
library media program are determined by the educational goals
and objectives of the school.

Schools, like individuals, have unique characteristics, due to
historical circumstances, geography, pupil demographics, teaching and leadership styles, and a host of other factors. Although all
schools must maintain basic services, local and regional curricula
are reflected in program emphases. Specific priorities may
change over time within a single school, and they may differ between schools, between districts, and between state systems. In
one school, the library media program may be strongest in the areas of reading guidance and literature appreciation. In another,
resources and facilities could be concentrated on communication
skills and media production. One collection may specialize in the
performing arts, while another may support a toy lending or educational software evaluation project. The potential for developing
resources and services is limitless.

All effective school library media programs, whatever their
individual strengths, share common goals and principles in meeting the needs of users. These goals and principles provide the
school library media specialist with guidance in implementing a
program.

## The School Library Media Program's Contribution to the Educational Process

**The school library media program that is fully integrated into the school's curriculum is central to the learning process.** It is a critical element in students' intellectual development, promoting the love of learning and conveying the importance of using and evaluating information and ideas throughout life.

Developing the ability to think clearly, critically, and creatively depends on a steady flow of information—both from direct, firsthand perceptions and from perceptions filtered and communicated through media, which use the languages of voice, image, print, and gesture. The school library media program provides an abundance of appropriate learning resources in many formats. Critical thinking skills are also fostered when students are provided with opportunities to learn how to locate, analyze, evaluate, interpret, and communicate information and ideas. The library media specialist offers frequent, planned activities to instruct students and allow practice in the use of learning resources in varying formats.

In the school library media center, teachers and students learn to use new information technologies as teaching and learning tools. The library media specialist functions as an information "intermediary," helping students, teachers, and parents learn how to cope with the information explosion and how to exploit the possibilities of an extraordinarily rich information world.

A comprehensive school library media program offers students and teachers a variety of alternatives for accomplishing learning objectives. With appropriate materials, processes, and places, alternatives can be tailored to individual learning styles and abilities.

The program contributes to the student's individual growth and development. Self-concept and self-worth are enhanced when students, working independently or in small groups, use information resources and technologies successfully to meet their needs. These resources provide the flexibility necessary to help foster creativity and to help students discover and overcome challenges. Additionally, the resources available contribute to students' artistic and cultural development.

With a wide range of instructional materials, the center be-

comes an information laboratory, enabling students to explore and use information. The library media center provides a true "marketplace of ideas," where users find intellectual challenge as they evaluate and digest ideas. Through the program, students become familiar with the environment and services of a modern information agency, preparing them to use libraries and other information agencies throughout their lives.

## The School Library Media Program in Operation

Every school library media program is made up of two principal components. One component consists of the planned activities and services that assist students and staff in interacting with resources to facilitate learning and teaching. The other embraces the information, personnel, equipment, and space resources needed to support these activities and services.

### Activities and Services Supporting Teaching and Learning

Within the school library media center, students and teachers engage in many different learning activities. The term *school li-*

*brary media center* conjures up pictures of: students deeply engrossed in reading—at a table or comfortably sprawled out in a "reading corner"; students using various information resources, either books or computerized information services; a circle of younger children enjoying a dramatic reading of a story; or a group of students working with the library media specialist in producing a video presentation.

In the library media center classroom, a media production class is planning a video presentation to a Spanish class. Elsewhere in the library media center, a teacher is making arrangements for the broadcast of a videotape in the classroom and conferring with one of the school library media specialists on the best way to present information on the DNA molecule. A teacher seeks another library media specialist's help in identifying materials to be used by a class that is scheduled to visit the school library media center. The teacher wishes to try a new approach to teaching a difficult concept and will work with the school library media specialist to design an appropriate learning activity.

A complete picture of a school library media center is one in which all these activities—and more—occur. The school library media program includes the sharing of ideas and stories through storytelling, slide and video productions, and dramatic presentations. Students of all ages use modern video equipment and simple cameras to create visual images to convey information and to communicate with others. Students teach each other and confer with the teacher or library media specialist as they work in the center on such learning projects. Teachers, the school library media specialist, and students encourage each other to explore new materials and try out different sources of information.

The library media staff members provide instruction in using materials and equipment through formal presentations that introduce new materials or teach specific access skills such as electronic searching. Less formal instruction occurs as students request help from the school library media specialist or are offered help when a need for assistance is observed. On personal computers, students use tutorial programs as well as word processing and graphics software.

School library media specialists hold regular planning meetings with individual teachers and teaching teams. Working collaboratively, they design instructional units and identify potential

resources for purchase. Curriculum planning, the design of learning activities, and the development of locally produced teaching
materials occur on an ongoing basis.

The library media specialist constantly engages in various
"intermediary" activities to ensure that users are able to gain intellectual as well as physical access to the information they need. As
the primary link between users and information, the school library
media specialist provides many kinds and levels of assistance.

All of these activities are aimed at improving individual and
group learning. They provide the motivation, practice, and opportunities necessary to foster independent inquiry and self-
directed learning. And perhaps most important of all, they are
carried out in an atmosphere that encourages users to feel excited
about information and ideas and competent in their use.

### Resources and Spaces Needed to Support
### Learning and Teaching

Effective learning and teaching dictate that information resources and specialized spaces be both sufficient and readily
available. School library media programs require spaces designed to accommodate learning activities, to house and display

materials, and to provide for the distribution and delivery of information and learning resources to all parts of the school building.
Library media specialists work both to ensure that learning resources can be used throughout the building and to create spaces
that encourage their use.

The center itself attracts students and is organized so that
many activities can occur simultaneously. In the school library
media center, some students seek out a quiet place to study alone.

Others prefer to work together, using a conference room for a small group discussion or practice for a debate. The school library media center has adjacent teaching space so that formal instruction can be given to students in an environment conducive to effective learning. Teachers make use of areas set aside for them to study, to prepare and reproduce teaching materials, or to hold meetings or conferences. Media production areas allow students and teachers to develop film, make audiotapes, create video productions, and view videotapes or films.

Students have convenient access to all media. The open areas around bookstacks, audiovisual materials, current periodicals, paperback displays, and reference counters make it possible for physically impaired students to reach materials. Displays and promotional materials encourage students to explore new sources of information and find materials for curricular and recreational reading, viewing, and listening.

Users have access to a vast range and variety of information resources in the school library media center, throughout the school, and beyond. Computer networks provide access to nationwide and even worldwide information resources. The school library media center collection contains general and special collections of heavily used print and nonprint resources. In addition to emphasizing materials which specifically relate to various school subjects, the collection also houses materials that provide opportunities to pursue individual interests.

Information is available through many formats, including books and periodicals, microforms, computer software, film and video, CD-ROM databases, and others. Access to this information is provided through printed and computerized indexes, catalogs, and other searching assistance programs. These inquiry aids, in conjunction with personal assistance from library media specialists, provide convenient and effective intellectual access to the world of information resources.

Specific guidelines for the resources and equipment needed for an effective school library media program are described in chapter 5; those for the physical and spatial requirements of the school library media center are included in chapter 6.

## Partnerships for a Successful School Library Media Program

**An effective school library media program depends on the collaborative efforts of all those who are responsible for student learning.** The coordination of curriculum development and implementation with the resources of the school library media center, and the application of principles of information access to the content of the curriculum provide the basis for an effective program. In effect, all members of the educational community, including teachers, principals, students, and library media specialists, become partners in a shared goal—providing successful learning experiences for all students.

### The Principal

The principal, working under the district superintendent, is the primary instructional leader in the school. Principals must be knowledgeable about resource-based learning and the importance of the school library media program. The principal is responsible for communicating the expectations for the school library media program to all the staff and for assuring that the school library media specialist serves as a member of the teaching team. Working together with teachers and the school library media specialists to set clear goals and provide methods of evaluating progress, the principal can facilitate the full integration of the school library media program into the curriculum.

As the chief building administrator, the principal ensures that the school library media program has adequate resources to carry out its mission and provides the necessary clerical help to allow the library media specialists to serve in a professional role. The principal also supports that role by structuring the use of the library media center flexibly and allowing time for planning and curriculum work. In addition, the principal supports inservice activities that help teachers understand the use of varied information resources and how new technologies contribute to increased learning. The principal encourages the development of relationships with other community agencies so that teachers use material and human resources within the community, as well as those of the school library media center, in structuring learning activities for their students.

### The Teacher

In a resource-based instructional program, the teacher identifies the learning needs of the students and develops teaching units to meet them. This development includes the selection of a variety of teaching strategies, the use of appropriate resource materials, and the evaluation of student achievement. The classroom teacher works with the school library media specialist, who is also a teacher, to assure effective use of all appropriate formats of instructional materials in students' learning experiences. In addition, the classroom teacher works cooperatively with the library media staff to encourage and assist students in the production of media.

Part of the teacher's role in using information and instructional resources as the basis for learning includes the cooperative development and teaching of an information skills curriculum. Classroom teachers and library media specialists work together in developing skills for learning throughout life, including appreciation and enjoyment of all types of communication media.

### The Student

The student is a partner in the learning process—no less than the principal, the teacher, and the library media specialist—and, as such, should have opportunities for regular participation in planning for school library media program activities. Students may serve on advisory councils and help in planning, evaluating, and promoting school library media services. Whenever possible, students should have opportunities to participate in the selection

and evaluation of materials, in the development of policies for use of the school library media center and its materials, and in the creation of new activities that serve learning needs.

### The Library Media Specialist

As partners in the learning process, library media specialists provide the necessary human link between a well-developed library media program and the users served by the program. As such, they translate the goals presented in the mission statement into vibrant, inspiring learning experiences. Library media specialists bring to the school community expert knowledge about the world of information and ideas in all their forms. The three roles of the library media specialist—information specialist, teacher, and instructional consultant—are described in detail in chapter 3.

---

## Guidelines for School Library Media Program Development

The school library media program plays a critical role in teaching and learning activities.

The library media program is fully integrated into the curriculum, serving the school's educational goals and objectives by providing access to information and ideas for the entire school community.

The principal, the library media specialist, teachers and students work together to ensure that the program contributes fully to the educational process in the school.

The library media program offers both traditional resources and new technologies as teaching and learning tools.

The program is housed in a school library media center that provides adequate and appropriate space for all the resources and activities of the program.

The library media center is convenient, comfortable, and aesthetically inviting.

## Selected Readings

Baker, Phil. *The Library Media Program and the School.* Littleton, Colo.: Libraries Unlimited, 1984.

   Baker's view of the function of the library media program in the school.

Charter, Jody Beckley. *Case Study Profiles of Six Exemplary Public High School Library Media Programs.* Ph.D. dissertation, Florida State University, 1982.

   A study of both the services, programs, and the personalities of exemplary library media specialists.

Haycock, Ken. "Services of School Resource Centers." *Emergency Librarian* 13, no. 1 (September/October, 1985): 28–29.

   Haycock advocates that the library media center should be an integral part of the curriculum processes in the school.

Loertscher, David V., May Lein Ho, and Melvin M. Bowie. "Exemplary Elementary Schools and Their Library Media Centers: A Research Report." *School Library Media Quarterly* 15, no. 3 (Spring 1987): 147–153.

*Partners in Action: The Library Resource Centre in the School Curriculum.* Toronto: Ontario Ministry of Education, 1983.

   One of the finest and clearest statements of the role of the library media program in the curriculum of the school.

Schmidt, William D. *Learning Resources Programs That Make a Difference: A Source of Ideas and Models from Exemplary Programs in the Field.* Washington, D.C.: AECT, 1987.

   Schmidt surveys programs in schools and colleges that are exemplary in terms of educational technology.

Seager, Andrew J., Sarah J. Roberts, and Carol Z. Lincoln. *Check This Out: Library Programs That Work.* Washington, D.C.: U.S. Department of Education, 1987.

   Descriptions of sixty-two outstanding library media program components selected for dissemination through the National Diffusion Network.

Vandergrift, Kay E. and Jane Anne Hannigan. "Elementary School Library Media Centers as Essential Components in the Schooling Process: An AASL Position Paper." *School Library Media Quarterly* 14, no. 4 (Summer 1986) 171–173.

   An important and succinct statement about the purpose of the elementary school library media center, followed by an extensive bibliography.

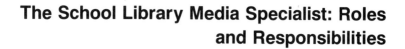

# The School Library Media Specialist: Roles and Responsibilities

A fundamental responsibility of the library media specialist is to provide the leadership and expertise necessary to ensure that the library media program is an integral part of the instructional program of the school. To carry out the mission of the program, the library media specialist performs the following separate but overlapping roles to link the information resources and services of the library media program to the information needs and interests of the school's students and staff:

**information specialist**
**teacher**
**instructional consultant.**

Through these roles, library media specialists provide:

- access to information and ideas by assisting students and staff in identifying information resources and in interpreting and communicating intellectual content
- formal and informal instruction in information skills, the production of materials, and the use of information and instructional technologies
- recommendations for instructional planning to individual teachers as well as assistance in schoolwide planning of curricular and instructional activities.

Library media specialists frequently perform the three roles of information specialist, teacher, and instructional consultant in concert with each other to establish the essential information and idea base required for formal and informal learning. However, the degree of emphasis on any one role may vary from school to school, depending on the particular school's goals, priorities, and resources.

## The Library Media Specialist as Information Specialist

The role of the library media specialist as information specialist is extremely important because an individual's success in the next century will depend, to a large extent, upon the ability to access, evaluate, and use information. Providing access to information and resources is a long-standing responsibility of school library media specialists. However, the importance and complexity of this function have increased dramatically in recent years, in part, due to the revolution in information and instructional technologies. While this revolution offers unprecedented opportunities for improved access to information and ideas, it also poses a number of issues for the library media specialist.

### *Providing Access to the Library Media Center*

The materials in the school library media collection and the expertise of the center's staff are central to meeting users' daily

learning and information needs. Therefore, it is necessary that both be readily available to the school community throughout and beyond the entire school day. Class visits to the library media center are scheduled to facilitate use at the point of need. Any functions that restrict or interfere with open access to all resources, including scheduled classes on a fixed basis, must be avoided to the fullest extent possible.

In developing service patterns, library media specialists advocate extended hours before and after school, along with special evening, weekend, or summer hours. School districts must plan to compensate, provide compensatory time, or determine other locally acceptable arrangements for library media personnel on a pro rata basis comparable to that of other instructional personnel who provide similar extended hours' services.

### Providing Adequate Resources

The information needs of users change continuously. Library media specialists determine users' needs through formal and informal assessment, and implement programs and procedures to identify and alert users to services and resources that respond to their needs. Users are informed on a regular basis of new acquisitions, relevant periodical articles, new programs, and events of interest in the community.

The school library media center collection must be adequate to meet the changing needs of the students and staff. The collection includes both resources that are housed on the individual campus and access to those that are outside the school. Library media specialists are responsible for working with teachers to ensure that the resources selected meet the specific goals and objectives of the curriculum and the interests of the students and staff. Additionally, they must work with administrators to ensure that adequate funding is available to keep the collection current and meet the changing needs of the instructional program.

Library media specialists facilitate access to resources outside the school by networking with other information agencies, borrowing or renting specialized materials, and/or using telecommunication devices to transmit information.

*Providing Assistance in Locating Information*

School library media specialists function as intermediaries responsible for guiding users through today's complex world of information resources. They have a responsibility to assist and guide students and staff as they seek to use and understand the resources and services of the program.

Frequently students need assistance in defining what they need to know, what resources might address that need, and when and how to select and use various search strategies. The objective is to help them to develop a systematic mode of inquiry to gain physical and intellectual access to information and ideas that reflect diversity of experiences, opinions, and social and cultural perspectives. The library media specialist, working as a partner with the teacher, is responsible for ensuring that students develop these abilities. Sometimes library media personnel work with individual students to construct search strategies: at other times, small groups receive this assistance.

Skills to be mastered include manual searching of appropri-

ate reference tools and computer searching of online and local databases and electronic catalogs; use of equipment to access information in various formats; and, most importantly, the development of higher-order thinking skills for the organization, evaluation, and use of information and ideas as an integral part of the content and objectives of the school's curriculum.

Of course, at times it is appropriate for the library media staff to provide information for students without leading them through the search process. Professional judgment is used to determine when to provide information directly to students and when to refer students to information sources.

### Guiding Users in the Selection of Appropriate Resources

Library media specialists serve as advisors to students as they select appropriate resources for personal and academic needs. Library media specialists provide help that is tailored to the needs and skills of the individual student and, when appropriate, review student interests, capabilities, and motivational level. Such guidance is based on an in-depth knowledge of:

- the complete range of educational materials, their potential uses, and their relationships to each other
- the psychological, social, and intellectual development of children and adolescents
- techniques for determining individual needs and interests and for matching them with appropriate materials
- approaches for presenting materials that make reading, listening, and viewing meaningful and attractive.

Teachers, library media specialists, administrators, and parents all share responsibility for the ongoing growth of students' reading, listening, and viewing skills. Through coordinated, cooperative programs in these areas, students are encouraged to take pleasure in learning, to develop lifelong reading, listening, and viewing habits, and to understand the need to be skilled in all modes of communication.

### Developing Flexible Policies for the Use of Resources

Circulation, loan, and use policies and services enable students and teachers to use materials and equipment throughout the school and at home. Policies must ensure maximum access; only in exceptional cases are materials and equipment barred for loan outside the library media center.

The rights of users to confidentiality and unrestricted access to information are protected by policies and procedures. When appropriate, the library media specialists work with the school or district administrators to secure necessary adoption of policies by the local board of education. Library media specialists are responsible for ensuring that regulations do not impede or prevent access (e.g., fees, interlibrary loan restrictions, online database costs). Students who receive instruction at remote sites, whether for physical or geographical reasons, must have access to information and materials through electronic transmissions, interlibrary loans, mobile collections, and other circulation procedures.

### Providing Retrieval Systems

An accurate and efficient retrieval system is essential for gaining access to information. All instructional materials that are not classroom specific (i.e., laboratory kits, worksheets, etc.) are included in the retrieval system, including departmentally owned materials and locally produced media.

Traditional retrieval systems in book or card form are frequently supplemented with, and in some cases replaced by, microcomputers and online systems. These electronic catalogs make possible more convenient and extensive searching that widens the range of available resources within and beyond the school. Supplemental data sources include online searching of electronically stored databases, union catalogs of other information agencies' holdings, networks that provide access to specialists in various fields, and interlibrary loan networks. Library media specialists must be aware of the range of available retrieval systems, identify those that best meet the needs of the local program, and provide expertise in helping students and staff become knowledgeable and comfortable in their use.

## The Library Media Specialist as Teacher

### Instructing Students

Library media specialists are responsible for ensuring that skills, knowledge, and attitudes concerning information access, use, and communication are an integral part of the school curriculum. Information skills are important throughout life. In immediate terms, they provide a means of achieving learning objectives within the curriculum. In the long term, information skills have a direct impact on an individual's ability to deal effectively with a changing environment. Therefore, library media specialists work with teachers and administrators to define the scope and sequence of the information curriculum and ensure its integration throughout the instructional program.

In some cases, library media specialists have primary responsibility for teaching information skills. In other cases, they reinforce and expand the concepts after other instructional personnel have laid the groundwork. However, library media specialists and teachers must work cooperatively to make certain that these learning activities take place and to reinforce them systematically. Mastery of these skills enables students to complete instructional tasks and explore personal interests.

Library media specialists help students build positive attitudes toward the use and communication of information and ideas. Students are encouraged to realize their potential as in-

formed citizens who think critically and solve problems, to observe rights and responsibilities relating to the generation and flow of information and ideas, and to appreciate the value of literature and recreational media in the life of an educated society.

Some major concepts that foster the building of these attitudes are:

- an understanding of the importance of critical thinking as an educational tool
- an appreciation of the link between critical reading, listening, and viewing skills and successful living
- an understanding of the importance of lifelong learning
- a recognition of the pleasure and fulfillment to be derived from using various media for both information and recreation
- an appreciation of the importance of adequate, freely available information sources in a democratic society
- a respect for and understanding of rights under the First Amendment of the U.S. Constitution
- an understanding of and respect for copyright, privacy, and other laws that promote access
- an understanding of the roles of the school library media center, the public library, and other information-providing agencies.

In addition, library media specialists teach students to understand the characteristics of each particular medium in which information and ideas are presented. With this knowledge, students develop both traditional means of communication—writing and speaking—and visual and auditory skills, gaining awareness that information and ideas are communicated in many different ways. Library media specialists teach students to recognize the effective and powerful means of communication at their disposal.

It is critical for library media specialists to convey to students the strengths and limitations of each medium; the appropriate use of a particular medium; and how to encode and decode ideas in each medium. Learning these concepts gives students the ability to evaluate information and ideas presented in various media formats. The library media specialist provides the instruction necessary to assist students to become effective producers and users of media.

### Instructing Educators and Parents

Library media specialists provide staff development opportunities for teachers and school administrators in the selection, use, evaluation, and production of media resources. These learning experiences update faculty on new and emerging technologies, and provide guidance for using and producing a variety of media. Library media personnel also keep instructional staff apprised of laws and policies pertaining to the use and communication of ideas and information.

The goal of such instruction is always to expand the methods available for meeting students' learning needs. When appropriate, the library media center staff enlists the support of outside experts in specialized fields. Teachers and administrators may expect library media specialists to keep them informed about inservice workshops, courses, meetings, and other professional activities that relate to their interests.

Instruction for parents assists them in sharing reading, listening, and viewing experiences with their children. Parents play an important role in instilling in children and adolescents the importance of lifelong learning and in developing in them an appreciation of all media. School library media specialists help parents to recognize the needs of their children and to select appropriate materials to meet these needs. To reach this special audience, library media specialists deliver instruction in a variety of ways, including personal consultations, workshops, and speaking engagements for civic and governmental organizations.

## The Library Media Specialist as Instructional Consultant

School library media specialists are consultants to teachers as they employ a wide range of resources and teaching methodologies to meet the intellectual and developmental needs of students. Library media specialists are teachers and have a broad knowledge base that includes an understanding of media, the application of media to the learning process, the needs of students for information sources, and instructional strategies.

As an instructional consultant, the library media specialist has the following responsibilities:

- participating in school, district, departmental, and grade-level curriculum design and assessment projects
- helping teachers develop instructional activities
- providing expertise in the selection, evaluation, and use of materials and emerging technologies for the delivery of information and instruction
- translating curriculum needs into library media program goals and objectives.

### Curriculum Development

Curriculum development is the process that identifies educational goals and sets realistic expectations for learners. Through this process, faculty, administrators, and community representatives determine what will be taught.

In view of the interrelationship between the curriculum and the resources and services of the school library media program, library media specialists should be members of both the building and the district curriculum development teams. Membership on curriculum committees provides library media personnel with opportunities to advise the educational staff on the selection, acquisition, use, and evaluation of specific media and media services as they pertain to meeting learning objectives. The library media staff also keeps instructional staff apprised of trends and directions affecting curriculum design. The library media specialists' contributions to curriculum development are enhanced by insights acquired in serving all grades, content areas, and age levels.

By serving on curriculum committees, library media specialists ensure that information access skills—including higher-order thinking skills—are incorporated into subject areas. Involvement in the curriculum development process also permits library media specialists to provide advice on the use of a variety of instructional strategies, such as learning centers and problem-solving software, which may be effective in communicating content to students.

### Instructional Development

Instructional development is the systematic process that guides the planning, implementation, and evaluation of instruction in the individual classroom. A student's success in acquiring knowledge, skills, and positive learning attitudes depends largely upon the effectiveness of instructional activities.

Because of the multiplicity of roles and functions that are associated with instruction, it is difficult for the classroom teacher to acquire all of the competencies necessary to meet individual students' learning needs. The increasing complexity in the instructional process requires a partnership between classroom teachers and library media specialists in instructional development.

Using a systematic process, library media specialists contribute to the development of instructional activities in the school by participating in the design, production, implementation, and evaluation of complete instructional units. Throughout the instructional development process, library media specialists assist classroom teachers with the following tasks:

developing unit objectives that build viewing, listening, reading, and critical thinking skills and that respond to student needs, as determined by a formal assessment process

analyzing learner characteristics that will influence design and use of media in an instructional unit

evaluating present learning activities and advising appropriate changes

organizing the instructional plan, indicating when, where, how, and by whom activities will be presented

examining and identifying resources that may be helpful in teaching the unit

identifying materials that must be produced locally or adapted from other materials, within copyright guidelines, and determining how they will be developed

identifying logistical problems that must be addressed in order to implement the instructional plan

securing equipment, materials, and services required to implement the learning unit

assisting in the delivery of unit content and activities

determining types of assessment, especially when learning alternatives include various types of media

evaluating and modifying learning activities, based on feedback gained from observation and interaction with students.

As consultants throughout the instructional development process, library media personnel play a key role in effective instruction. Library media specialists must assume leadership roles in developing opportunities to work with teachers. Although library media professionals provide varying levels of assistance to teachers, the greater the level of involvement, the more effectively the library media specialists contribute to the success of teaching and learning activities.

### Use of Technology

Curriculum and instructional development, like all other aspects of education, continue to be influenced significantly by major, ongoing technological advancements. The resulting array of complex instructional and educational technologies can overwhelm educators seeking ways to integrate the many existing and emerging information and instructional technologies into the school's curriculum.

The revolution in information and instructional technologies provides unprecedented opportunities for improving access to information and ideas. These new opportunities for access challenge school library media specialists to be aware of new developments, recognize those appropriate for their library media

programs, and provide the leadership and expertise for their incorporation into the instructional program of the school.

Library media specialists must be responsible for assessing and promoting effective use of instructional technologies. They must play a leading role on the school's technology planning team because they are educated to evaluate, select, and manage the technologies that make information and ideas available in a wide variety of formats. As a member of the team, the library media specialist provides an assessment of the potential impact of specific technologies. Once a decision is made to adopt a particular information or instructional technology, library media specialists assume responsibility for instructing faculty and students in its optimal use.

## Guidelines for Fulfilling Roles and Responsibilities

### Information Specialist

Library media specialists make resources available to students and teachers through a systematically developed collection within the school and through access to resources outside the school.

Access to the library media center collection is provided by an accurate and efficient retrieval system that uses the expanding searching capabilities of the computer.

Students receive assistance in identifying, locating, and interpreting information housed in and outside the library media center.

Students and teachers have access to the library media center and to qualified professional staff throughout the school day. Class visits are scheduled flexibly to encourage use at point of need.

Policies and procedures ensure that access to information is not impeded by fees, loan restrictions, or online searching charges.

Teachers, students, parents, and administrators are informed of new materials, equipment, and services that meet their information needs.

Students at remote sites are provided with access to information.

## Teacher

The information curriculum is taught as an integral part of the content and objectives of the school's curriculum.

The information curriculum includes instruction in accessing, evaluating, and communicating information and in the production of media.

Library media specialists and teachers jointly plan, teach, and evaluate instruction in information access, use, and communication skills.

Assistance is provided in the use of technology to access information outside the library media center.

Teachers and other adults are offered learning opportunities related to new technologies, use and production of a variety of media, and laws and policies regarding information.

Library media specialists use a variety of instructional methods with different user groups and demonstrate the effective use of newer media and technologies.

## Instructional Consultant

Library media specialists participate in building, district, department, and grade-level curriculum development and assessment projects on a regular basis.

Library media specialists offer teachers assistance in using information resources, acquiring and assessing instructional materials, and incorporating information skills into the classroom curriculum.

Library media specialists use a systematic instructional development process in working with teachers to improve instructional activities.

Library media specialists provide leadership in the assessment, evaluation, and implementation of information and instructional technologies.

## Selected Readings

Anderson, Pauline H. *Library Media Leadership in Academic Secondary Schools.* Hamden, Conn.: Library Professional Publications/ Shoestring Press, 1985.

The role of the library media specialist working in the private or academically oriented high school.

Callison, Daniel. "School Library Media Programs and Free Inquiry Learning." *School Library Journal* 32, no. 6 (February 1986): 20–24.

Callison provides a method for conducting resource-based teaching as a cooperative activity between the teacher and the library media specialist that will encourage growth and development of inquiry learning (student questioning and discovery of information).

Craver, Kathleen W. "The Changing Instructional Role of the High School Library Media Specialist: 1950–84." *School Library Media Quarterly* 14, no. 4 (Summer 1986): 183–192.

Craver provides a summary of the research literature that documents the changing responsibilities of the library media specialist.

Dalbotten, Mary, ed. *Model Learner Outcomes for Educational Media and Technology.* White Bear Lake, Minn.: Minnesota Department of Education, 1986.

One of the most specific definitions and guides for the roles of the library media specialist. Can be used both as a guide for writing job descriptions and as an evaluative tool.

Dick, Walter and Lou Carey. *The Systematic Design of Instruction.* 2nd ed. Glenview, Ill.: Scott, Foresman, 1985.

A basic book describing the process of instructional development.

*Instruction in Library Media Skills: A Supplement to a Guide to School Library Media Programs.* Hartford, Conn.: Connecticut Department of Education, 1984.

An accompanying manual to the Connecticut state standards that not only provides an exemplary skills continuum but also provides sample units of instruction in which those skills are integrated.

Kemp, Jerrold E. *The Instructional Design Process.* New York: Harper & Row, 1985.

A basic text that describes systematic instructional planning.

Kuhlthau, Carol Collier. "A Process Approach to Library Skills Instruction." *School Library Media Quarterly* 13, no. 1 (Winter 1985): 35–44.

Kuhlthau explores the stages of research.

Mancall, Jacqueline C., Shirley L. Aaron, and Sue A. Walker. "Educating Students to Think: The Role of the School Library Media Program." *School Library Media Quarterly* 15, no. 1 (Fall 1986): 18–27.

Rosenfield, Sylvia. *Instructional Consultation.* Hillsdale, N.J.: Lawrence Erlbaum Associates, 1987.

Instructional development from the point of view of the school psychologist.

Turner, Philip. *Helping Teachers Teach.* Littleton, Colo.: Libraries Unlimited, 1986.

Turner translates the formal instructional design process into a practical method for school library media specialists.

Vandergrift, Kay E. *The Teaching Role of the School Media Specialist.* Chicago: American Library Association, 1979.

One of the earliest and most significant documents about the teaching responsibilities of the library media specialist.

Wilkens, Lea-Ruth C. *Supporting K-5 Reading Instruction in the School Library Media Center.* Chicago: American Library Association, 1984.

Suggestions for the involvement of school library media professionals in the teaching of reading.

# Leadership, Planning, and Management

The mission and goals of the library media program are translated into action through positive leadership, sound planning, and effective and efficient management of human and physical resources. Leadership is the crucial factor in creating a quality library media program that is an integral part of the school curriculum. Effective leadership articulates the vision of such a program with enthusiasm and confidence, inspiring others to identify with and support its goals.

Managing the library media program involves a number of specific, interrelated responsibilities, including planning and evaluating, organizing and supervising, budgeting, staffing, and promoting all aspects of the program. Planning is the basis for all other management functions and, if it is to be effective, must include evaluation as an integral part of the process. Effective management entails developing program goals and priorities and translating them into action.

## Leadership

Leadership requires a clear understanding of the present library media program and a broad vision of its potential. Technological change and the proliferation of information in new and different formats have special implications for decisions relating to future resources, services, and activities. Demographic trends and socioeconomic forces present new issues and needs that must be continually addressed in program planning and development.

The library media program's mission and goals must be evaluated periodically in terms of the current and potential impact these external changes will have on the needs of students and teachers.

Neither the schools, nor the library media programs within them, can operate in a vacuum. What happens within the school mirrors external expectations and constraints. Public pressure for accountability has caused schools to adopt more effective approaches to planning programs and allocating resources. Funding continues to be an issue, and decisions about which resources and programs to provide must be based on careful analysis of educational needs. As needs change, teaching and learning resources must be reorganized, reallocated and/or expanded to provide for new and different learning alternatives.

The leadership and commitment of the library media professional are crucial factors in developing credibility for the library media program as an integral part of teaching and learning in the school. The library media specialist, the principal, and the district director of library media programs—working individually and as a team—create an atmosphere that inspires others to identify with and support the goals of the program. These individuals must jointly develop library media program goals, establish priorities, and allocate the resources necessary to accomplish the mission.

The building-level library media specialist must assume leadership in establishing and nurturing this administrative partnership, as well as in creating an instructional partnership among students, faculty, and the community. To fulfill these responsibilities and to anticipate and articulate the information needs of the school community, the library media specialist must have high levels of professional expertise, credibility, and communication skills, maintained through continuing professional development.

The energy, enthusiasm, and interpersonal skills that library media personnel demonstrate in day-to-day interactions with people—students, teachers, administrators, parents, and the community—create a positive image of the program. A high level of effective services and activities, designed to meet specific needs of individual users and overall curriculum needs, develops the credibility necessary to ensure moral and financial support for translating program goals into action.

## Planning

Planning is central to every facet of program development and implementation. It is a continuing process, rather than a single step or one-time project, and is subject to ongoing evaluation and revision. Successful planning requires the allocation of adequate time and resources and the establishment of a realistic timetable. It also requires that the purposes for planning and the outcomes expected be established and clearly articulated. Information and recommendations from previous planning and evaluation efforts must be reviewed early in the process.

Planning is initiated at the district or school level by either administrative or library media personnel. At the school level, the library media specialist initiates and directs the planning activities under the direction of the principal. Because planning is a cooperative effort, involving library media professionals and other members of the school community, it is important to determine the level of involvement and specific responsibilities of different individuals and groups. Extensive participation of teachers, students, and administrators is vital to the process.

A sound planning process:

- defines the library media program mission and goals
- shapes the roles and responsibilities of the library media specialist
- gives direction to the allocation, organization, and management of physical and human resources
- focuses attention on program effectiveness and efficiency
- identifies alternative activities and services for current and potential users
- establishes priorities for allocating limited resources
- promotes organizational, program, and individual accountability
- provides information for evaluating individual decisions and actions as well as programs
- orients the program toward future possibilities while preparing for current realities.

### Beginning the Planning Process

Before initiating the planning activities, preliminary decisions must be made. Answers to the following basic questions provide a basis for organizing the planning activities:

What are the purposes for planning?

What products are expected from the planning effort? How will they be communicated? To which groups?

Who should be involved in the planning process?

What are the specific responsibilities of the various participants?

How much time will be required for the planning process? For the director? For participants?

What resources are required to support the planning effort?

When will the planning process be completed?

How will the planning process, activities, results, and recommendations be evaluated?

Who will be responsible for collecting data?

What data will be required?

### Defining the Program Mission, Goals, and Objectives

The library media program's mission is a concise statement of its general purpose. The mission statement guides decisions in planning and communicates the program's focus to administrators, educators, students, and the community. The mission statement in chapter 1 provides an example that may be used in developing a local mission statement.

Setting goals and objectives for the program helps to translate the mission into more specific statements of desired results and targets toward which to work. Goals are long-range (e.g., 3–5 years), broad statements of desired ends. They provide a framework for the objectives, which are specific targets within each of the goals. Objectives are also time limited, but they are usually short range and readily measurable or verifiable. The goals and objectives of the library media center program all work to support the overall educational goals and priorities of the school and district.

Collectively, the mission statement, goals, and objectives provide the foundation for the development of implementation strategies and activities. Close collaboration between the library media staff and the principal is necessary to identify specific implementation activities related to each objective. Responsibility for carrying out these activities must be assigned to appropriate staff members. Regular reporting of the status of different activities should be scheduled, in order to assess the degree to which they achieve the desired goals and objectives.

### Collecting Needed Information

Identifying and collecting the information necessary for effective planning is crucial. Too little information can seriously hamper or mislead the planning effort; too much information can be overwhelming, as well as costly in terms of time and effort expended. All data collected must be both relevant and reliable. To determine whether a specific type of information should be collected, consider how it will be used and how important it is in making decisions about the program. The kind and quality of data collected determine, in large measure, the quality of the entire planning effort.

Some kinds of data—such as number and cost of materials and equipment held and acquired, numbers of students and staff, and descriptions of facilities—are readily available. Other kinds of important data must be gathered specifically for the planning effort. These include use of staff time in performing various activities and services, and data regarding the needs of students and teachers. Data regarding accomplishments of library media programs (program outputs), although more difficult to collect, provide valuable information for planning program improvements in the following areas:

1. How effectively does the program provide for information access, services, and activities required to meet individual and instructional program needs? (How well is the program doing?)
2. How efficiently does the library media staff use information resources, facilities, skills, time, and effort to link students and teachers to the information and ideas they need? (Is the program doing the right things?)

### Implementing Planning Recommendations

The data collected are analyzed and used in developing the policies, procedures, and activities to implement the program defined in the mission, goals, and objectives statements. Translating the statements into action involves careful analysis of existing physical and human resources and the current program's activities and services. Difficult decisions must be made as new activities are examined in terms of their impact on existing resources and programs:

> Which activity best relates to the goals and objectives statements developed by the planning team?
>
> What amount and kinds of physical and human resources will be required to carry out the activity?
>
> Are these resources available?
>
> Will existing resources need to be reallocated or reorganized?
>
> Will additional resources need to be provided? At what cost?
>
> Does the library media staff have the competencies necessary to carry out the activity?
>
> Must staff time be reallocated to implement the new activity? Is this feasible?
>
> What will be the positive or negative impact on current activities and services?

When implementation of the planning committee's recommendations will have a negative impact on existing library media program activities, choices must be made. The planning team, or advisory committee, must participate in the analysis of alternatives and in the final decisions about program priorities. Credibility of the planning process depends on this crucial step.

The school library media staff, in consultation with administrative personnel and the advisory committee, implement the recommendations resulting from the planning process. Continual communication is essential as program activities are implemented.

### Evaluating the Library Media Program

The library media program must be evaluated systematically in order to review overall goals and objectives in relation to user and instructional needs, and to assess the efficiency and effectiveness of specific activities. Participation by the administrative staff and advisory committee in this assessment is essential to ensure their continued awareness and support. The evaluation process should answer questions such as:

> What proportion of the total school population (students and staff) is being served?
>
> What identifiable subgroups are being served? In what ways? With what frequency?
>
> With what frequency and effectiveness do the library media specialists participate in instructional planning with teachers?
>
> How effectively can students use information resources to meet specific learning objectives?
>
> With what frequency and effectiveness do teachers use library media resources and activities to accomplish classroom objectives?
>
> How well are the library media program's objectives being met?

Regular and systematic evaluation provides the basis for decisions regarding the development, continuation, modification, or elimination of policies and procedures, activities, and services, and begins anew the planning process. The allocation of resources and the quality and consistency of staff performance are of primary importance in program review.

## Management

Every library media program must have a designated head of the program. In programs that have only one professional position, the library media specialist is considered the head. This individual is responsible for developing and implementing the wide range of policies and procedures necessary for the efficient and effective operation of the program. These must be developed and implemented within the context of overall school district policies and procedures. Some policies, such as those dealing with collection development and selection of resources, must be formally adopted by the local board of education. Others of more limited scope, such as those dealing with circulation or hours of operation, may be created and implemented within the individual building. In all cases, however, policies and procedures are designed to ensure maximum access to the full range of information resources and services for students and staff. Policies and procedures must be clearly articulated and widely communicated to the school community.

Another important component of effective library media program management is the recording and reporting of a wide variety of data regarding holdings, services, use, and finances. The head of the library media program uses these data to prepare periodic and annual reports that document the impact of the library media program on the overall educational program of the school. The annual report provides an opportunity to assess progress, to determine strengths and weaknesses, and to redefine program goals for the coming year.

### Budgeting

Budgeting is the financial aspect of planning and managing the library media program. The library media center budget supports the philosophy of the school library media program in quantitative terms, just as the overall school budget supports the educational philosophy of the community it serves. The budget process involves identifying specific program goals and objectives through the planning process, specifying the physical and human resources required to accomplish these, and communicating the financial requirements for supplying these resources. State guidelines and regional accreditation standards provide specific suggestions regarding budgetary requirements and trends within the respective state and region.

The director of the district library media program is responsible, through established administrative channels, for the design, formulation, justification, administration, and evaluation of the library media budget in the district. The district program director assumes a leadership role in representing and communicating the resource requirements and needs of both district and building level programs. Regional and state standards for library media resources must be considered in preparing district- and building-level library media budgets.

The library media budget includes operating funds for ongoing program support and capital outlay for majority expenditures such as: construction of new or remodeled facilities; acquisition of initial materials collections, equipment, and furniture for new schools; or installation of new technologies in new or existing schools.

At the building level, the head of the school library media program develops the individual school's library media budget, in cooperation with the principal and the district program director. The library media advisory committee should be included in the budget process; its active participation is an extension of the planning and evaluation process. It also encourages continued support for the jointly developed library media program goals and objectives.

Several factors must be considered in budget planning:
- changes in the kind and number of users served
- resource and service adaptations required for specialized populations, such as disabled, gifted, minority, or immigrant students
- curriculum or instructional changes
- characteristics of the collection, such as attrition by weeding, loss, and date
- general aging of the collection and equipment due to inadequate replacement
- increased costs of materials and equipment due to inflation
- changes in services due to new technology, such as database searching or television distribution systems.

Decision formulas that provide assistance in identifying factors to consider, as well as a process for calculating budgetary needs for materials and equipment, are included in Appendix B.

The budget presentations at both the school and district levels should emphasize the relationship of resources to program goals and objectives. Explanations and justifications of funding requests must be expressed in terms of how instructional and learning goals and objectives are realized through the library media program. The resources needed to achieve the specific goals and objectives of the library media program are then specified within this framework.

## Staffing

Staffing the library media program consists of defining personnel needs, securing qualified personnel, developing staff competencies to perform essential tasks, establishing standards of performance, and evaluating personnel performance. Library media professionals at the district and building levels assume leadership roles in accomplishing these staffing activities.

The heart of the library media program is the building-level staff. The key roles of the library media specialist in linking users to information and ideas have been discussed. Clerical and technical staff provide crucial support to each of the roles of the library media specialist. Support staff perform a myriad of important tasks that release the library media specialists to perform their professional roles. Library media program effectiveness and efficiency depend on the attitudes, competencies, and interpersonal skills of both professional and support staff.

The director of the district library media program must exert strong leadership in accomplishing all staffing activities. The district director, working cooperatively with administrative staff at both district and building levels, is responsible for coordinating efforts to recruit and select professional library media staff; to provide staff development opportunities; to prepare job descriptions; to establish performance standards; and to develop evaluation instruments to measure performance. The director works with the building administrator to clarify staff expectations and to assist with performance evaluation. The district director, through personal attitude and actions, sets the tone for developing positive relations among library media personnel, administrators, classroom teachers, and other district staff.

The library media specialists in the school, working within the context of district- and building-level policies and procedures, perform a variety of staffing activities. These responsibilities include participation in the selection, training, and evaluation of library media support staff in the individual school. Implicit in each of these activities is a continuing effort to establish positive relations between the library media professional and support staff. Firm and fair guidance of support staff is crucial. Equally important is the provision of frequent positive feedback for effective and efficient staff performance.

Formal job descriptions should be developed for all personnel in the school system. The district library media director assumes a leadership role in coordinating efforts to ensure that library media personnel—professional and support staff—clearly understand their roles, relationships, and responsibilities. The head of the school library media program provides leadership in translating the individual program goals and objectives into specific staff action. This leadership includes identifying specific responsibilities required for each activity and assigning tasks to building-level library media staff. Delegation of this responsibility to the head of the library media program is crucial to the effectiveness and efficiency of the operation of the program.

### Organizing and Directing the Program

Organizing and directing the library media program includes establishing an overall structure of relationships and responsibilities; identifying and defining the work to be done to meet goals and objectives; grouping work activities; and delegating authority to carry out responsibilities.

Library media specialists work within an overall district and school structure that has clearly defined authority relationships and responsibilities. Although these individuals often have little formal control over educational policies that have impact on services and working conditions, effective management of the library media program requires that they be knowledgeable about policy areas and have some understanding of the broader context of educational governance. Library media professionals at all levels must become knowledgeable about policy areas that restrict or limit the quality and quantity of activities and services for students and teachers. They must initiate efforts to make decision-makers aware of the negative impact of specific policies and procedures, and promote cooperative action to develop alternative policies and procedures.

### Promoting and Marketing the Program

Marketing the school library media program involves more than public relations. In today's climate of concern for effectiveness and accountability, there must be a clear understanding of the library media program's role in learning and teaching. The responsibility of the library media program staff in providing the information resources and services that undergird the total educational program must be clearly articulated. Library media personnel must effectively publicize available services and resources, visibly serve on school and district-wide committees, actively participate in community projects, and clearly demonstrate the importance of the library media program in education.

Consistent attention must be given to assessing changing needs of the curriculum and individual users. The total planning and evaluation process offers the opportunity for involvement of internal and external publics. The attitudes and interpersonal skills that library media staff demonstrate during interaction with these groups can bring positive visibility for library media programs. The partnership approach to program planning, in addition to making the program more responsive to user needs, creates shared commitment to library media program goals and an enhanced image for the overall program.

Ensuring consistent positive visibility for school and district library media program is of critical importance. Two-way communication between library media personnel and the school community promotes understanding and builds good will, cooperation, and support. The ultimate success of school library media programs depends, to a large extent, upon the level of understanding and support within the general school community for the mission, goals, and objectives of the program.

---

### Guidelines for Leadership, Planning, and Management

The mission, goals, and objectives of the library media program are clearly understood and fully supported by the administrative and educational staff, the students, and the community.

Responsibility for leading and managing the library media program is shared equally by the head of the building program, the principal, and the district library media director, who must jointly develop library media goals, establish priorities, and allocate the resources necessary to accomplish the mission.

Planning involves school and district library media program administrators, the library media staff, school administrators, teachers, students, and community members, as appropriate.

As part of the planning process, the library media program is evaluated on a regular basis to review overall goals and objectives in relation to user and instructional needs and to assess the efficiency and effectiveness of specific activities.

Program and personnel evaluations follow district-wide policies and procedures, focus on performance, and are based upon appropriately collected data.

The planning process results in periodic reports that emphasize and document progress toward stated goals and objectives.

The library media specialist, the principal, and the district library media coordinator cooperatively plan the library media center budget.

Sufficient funds are provided for the resources and personnel necessary to achieve the goals and objectives of the library media program.

A qualified library media program staff is fundamental to the implementation of effective school library media programs at the school and district levels. The quality and size of the professional and support staff are directly related to the range and level of services provided.

The selection, training, support, and evaluation of the library media staff are the key determinants in the success of the program.

The library media program must be promoted by library media personnel who demonstrate the importance of the library media program in education, publicize available services and resources to students and staff, serve on school and district-wide committees, and participate in community-wide projects.

## Selected Readings

Adams, Helen R. *School Media Policy Development: A Practical Process for Small Districts.* Littleton, Colo.: Libraries Unlimited, 1986. Includes sample policies on a wide range of topics.

*A Guide to School Library Media Programs.* Hartford, Conn.: Connecticut Department of Education, 1983.

One of the best examples of state standards.

Kulleseid, Eleanor R. *Beyond Survival to Power for School Library Media Professionals.* Hamden, Conn.: Library Professional Publications, 1985.

A revision of Kulleseid's dissertation; the author extrapolates from actual case histories recommendations on the politics and economics not merely of survival but also of empowerment for the building library media specialist and school district director.

Kulleseid, Eleanor R. and Carolyn A. Markuson. "Empowering the Professional: Alternative Visions of Leadership." *School Library Media Quarterly* 15, no. 4 (Summer 1987): 195–222.

A theme issue on leadership, which includes articles by the authors above as well as by Warren Bennis, Lillian Biermann Wehmeyer, Raymond D. Terrell, Donna Barkman, and Pauline H. Anderson.

Liesener, James W. *A Systematic Planning Process for School Media Programs.* Chicago: American Library Association, 1976.

Mancall, Jacqueline C. and M. Carl Drott. *Measuring Student Information Use: A Guide for School Library Media Specialists.* Littleton, Colo.: Libraries Unlimited, 1983.

Nickel, Mildred L. *Steps to Service: A Handbook of Procedures for the School Library Media Center,* rev. ed. Chicago: American Library Association, 1984.

A revised edition of the well-known library media manual.

*Procedures Manual for School Library Media Centers.* Oklahoma City: Oklahoma State Department of Education, 1982.

One of the best procedure manuals available. It is a compilation of many available manuals from all parts of the country.

Woolls, Blanche. *Grant Proposal Writing: A Handbook for School Library Media Specialists.* Westport, Conn.: Greenwood Press, 1987.

A manual for obtaining funding from outside district budgets.

Yesner, Bernice L. and Hilda L. Jay. *The School Administrator's Guide to Evaluating Library Media Programs.* Hamden, Conn.: Library Professional Publications, 1987.

Summary statements or points to consider as the principal looks for positive elements, negative elements, missing elements, and possible solutions to problems in school library media programs.

# Personnel

The success of any school library media program, no matter how well designed, depends ultimately on the quality and number of the personnel responsible for the program. A well-educated and highly motivated professional staff, adequately supported by technical and clerical staff, is critical to the endeavor.

As library media centers have evolved from mere warehouses for materials and equipment to dynamic information and resource programs, the need for increased professional staffing has grown significantly. Individual and small group interaction with students, along with increased consultation time with teachers, requires more effective and efficient use of all resources and services of the library media program. The availability and appropriate involvement of support staff not only allows library media specialists to function as professionals but also extends the opportunities for the professional staff to work with groups and individuals and enlarges the range of services provided by the library media program.

## Levels and Patterns of Staffing

Levels and patterns of staffing are dependent upon a number of variables. These variables include the size of the school, expectations of the faculty and students, the integration of the library media program into the curriculum, and the relationship of student learning to library media services and resources. The curriculum, organization (such as open school design, departmental management, etc.), physical plant, special student populations, general staffing of the school, and the services provided by district or regional library media programs also are critical elements in determining levels and patterns of staffing.

Although staffing patterns are developed to meet local needs, certain basic staffing requirements can be identified.

Staffing patterns must reflect the following principles:

1. **All students, teachers, and administrators in each school building at all grade levels must have access to a library media program provided by one or more certificated library media specialist working full-time in the school's library media center.**

2. **Both professional personnel and support staff are necessary for all library media programs at all grade levels.** Each school must employ at least one full-time technical assistant or clerk for each library media specialist. Some programs, facilities, and levels of service **will** require more than one support staff member for each professional.

3. **More than one library media professional is required in many schools.** The specific number of additional professional staff is determined by the school's size, number of students and of teachers, facilities, specific library media program components, and other features of the school's instructional program. A reasonable ratio of professional staff to teacher and student populations is required in order to provide for the levels of service and library media program development described in this document.

In large schools, it is appropriate to have a staff of professionals with a broad range of competencies and experiences. In this way, they provide complementary specializations. Additional professional staff is also required in schools with specialized resource areas and in schools where the physical facilities prohibit all library media program activities from originating in one general area. In such cases, the head of the school library media program ensures that specialists work together to avoid fragmenting or dividing the program.

In order to provide users with assistance at the time of need, professional staff in the library media center must be available to teachers, students, and others in the school community throughout the school day. Neither professional nor support staff should be assigned unrelated duties that interfere with effective operation of the library media program. Library media staff members are not assigned regularly scheduled content or subject area classes.

## Professional Staff

### Head of the School Library Media Program

Professional positions in the school library media program are always staffed by qualified and certificated school library media specialists. As noted in chapter 4, every library media program must have a designated head of the program. In programs that have only one professional position, the library media specialist is considered to be the head of the school library media program. The head of the school library media program is responsible for the planning, development, implementation, and overall evaluation of the entire program. This responsibility includes supervision of other professional staff—both library media and other specialists—and support staff.

Library media specialists are members of the faculty. The head of the library media program should be considered as a departmental chairperson, unit head, or lead teacher. With this title and position, the head of the library media program participates on standing curriculum and other school-wide committees. In some schools, the library media specialist is considered to be a part of the management team, in which case the position is equal to an assistant building administrator.

The head of the school library media program meets not only the qualifications for a school library media specialist but also any other degree or certification criteria required for appointment at that level. Additional academic and professional preparation is required as the program becomes more complex. The salary, fringe benefits, and working conditions of the head of the library media program are commensurate with others who have similar departmental responsibilities.

All library, media, and information services are coordinated by the head of the library media program. However, some administrative information systems, computer science departments, and/or departmental laboratories that house educational and information hardware may be more appropriately supervised by administrative, instructional, or technical staff other than the library media specialist.

### School Library Media Specialists

School library media specialists have a broad undergraduate education with a liberal arts background and hold a master's degree or equivalent from a program that combines academic and professional preparation in library and information science, education, management, media, communications theory, and technology. The academic program of study includes some directed field experience in a library media program, coordinated by a faculty member in cooperation with an experienced library media specialist. While there may be many practicing library media specialists who have only an undergraduate degree and whose job performance is outstanding, the master's degree is considered the entry-level degree for the profession.

The graduate degree is earned at colleges and universities whose programs are accredited by appropriate bodies such as the American Library Association (ALA), the National Council for the Accreditation of Teacher Education (NCATE), or state education agencies.

The following lists are guidelines for initial preparation programs, state and regional certification requirements, and continuing education/professional development activities in the profession:

*Library and Information Science:* library media center organization, administration, and management; print, nonprint, and hardware collection development; information technology, systems management, and information policy; network development and management; print and nonprint instructional and recreational materials for children and adolescents; library and information programming and services for children and adolescents; information needs and library services for special populations; and research and research methods.

*Education:* teaching and learning theories; psychology of learning and development in children, young persons, and adults; instructional development; curriculum development; learning needs of special populations; philosophy and social foundations; and research as applied to educational practices and the use of educational media and library services.

*Communications Theory:* interpersonal communications; information transfer by various media forms including mass media; and research as applied to library media programs.

*Technology:* telecommunications systems and services; computer systems and services; instructional design; basic and advanced forms of media production and use; administration of hardware and software systems; and facility design for proper media use.

Preparation programs for library media specialists place special emphasis on the need for continuing education throughout the professional career. These programs foster a positive attitude toward continual self-assessment and professional growth through both academic and nonacademic experiences. The learning experiences may be designed and delivered by colleges and universities, professional associations, regional and state agencies, or private consultants. Some continuing education experiences may also be developed by the individual library media specialist through systematic reading of professional literature, research and publication, hosting field experiences for library media specialist candidates, making presentations at professional conferences, and teaching as adjunct faculty in teacher/library media specialist preparation programs.

In addition to the competencies suggested by the list above, the library media specialist understands and demonstrates:

- a broad understanding of the role of the profession in society
- a commitment to ethical behavior
- strong leadership qualities
- a commitment to provide services to all members of the school community
- effective problem-solving, human relations, and interpersonal communication skills
- a commitment to continued learning and personal growth
- support for intellectual and academic freedom as provided in the First Amendment of the United States Constitution and the Library Bill of Rights
- active membership in professional associations at the local, regional, state, and national levels.

The library media specialist meets the state certification requirements for both the library media specialist and professional educator classifications. State guidelines for certification as a library media specialist should reflect the spirit and conceptual framework provided in this document.

### Other Media Professionals

Some schools require the services of other professional and technical staff. These professionals have additional certification in areas such as computer science and technology, instructional design, instructional television, media production, and information technology. They have academic preparation in educational theory and methodology, in addition to a degree in their specific disciplines.

## Support Staff

All library media programs, regardless of size, need an adequate level of support staff. The support staff works under the guidance and supervision of the professional staff, and provides services which free the professional staff to work directly and closely with students and faculty in the school. Support staff also may interact directly with the school community, but their primary responsibilities are more routine clerical and technical duties. School and district personnel, as appropriate, develop job descriptions and evaluation procedures for support personnel.

The support staff of the library media program consists of technicians, technical assistants, and clerks. They carry out carefully delineated duties for assisting users according to established procedures and perform specialized tasks involving materials and equipment. Support staff members require both a general knowledge of library media program activities and specific skills necessary for the performance of duties. All support staff members must also demonstrate positive human relations skills. Preparation for the position of technical assistant, technician, or clerk is by academic training in a program of studies at the undergraduate level, in a technical training institution, or by in-service training and on-the-job experience.

*Technicians* usually have some formal academic and technical training at the undergraduate or technical institution level, or experience in a specialized area of media production, maintenance, or use. These areas may include graphics and displays; photography; operation, maintenance and repair of instructional hardware; video and audio production and storage; installation and maintenance of video, audio, and other communications systems; and computer management and operation.

*Technical assistants* usually have a general background in library media program routines, acquired primarily from on-the-job experience and training, with limited formal training within an academic or technical institution. They may work directly with individuals and groups in activities coordinated by the library media specialist.

*Clerical staff members* usually have some formal training at the high school or technical institution level and experience in secretarial and basic business operations. They perform routine tasks in the areas of materials and hardware acquisition, file and

records maintenance, circulation, and use of materials and equipment. Some of the competencies that they demonstrate include: typing, word processing, and duplicating; filing, sorting, organizing, and shelving; maintaining records, inventorying, and accounting; and computer searching for cataloging and interlibrary loan.

## Adult Volunteers and Student Assistants

Additional assistance in the school library media center is often provided by volunteers and student aides. Volunteers—parents, retired persons, or other community members—are available in some schools to assist in specific areas of the library media program. They often possess unique talents, skills, and experiences, providing a number of services to supplement the work of the regular library media staff. However, **volunteers should not be considered as substitutes for trained, paid clerical and technical staff.** Duties essential for the efficient operation of the library media program must be performed by the center's support staff. Because the use of volunteers requires substantial supervision and training time from the professional staff, the cost and benefits must be carefully evaluated.

Student assistants may assist in the library media center before, during, or after regular school hours. These students can be valuable assets whose volunteer efforts contribute significantly to the library media program. They, in return, may receive valuable social, developmental, and educational experiences. As with all volunteers, students are not substitutes for paid support staff and must be carefully trained, supervised, and evaluated. Great care should be taken to ensure that students receive educational benefits from working in the media center.

## Evaluation of Library Media Personnel

Since library media specialists are members of the school's instructional staff, their evaluation is similar to the evaluation of other teaching professionals; however, instruments and procedures must be designed to recognize the unique responsibilities and contributions of the library media specialist to the total school program. The performance appraisal process requires clearly defined job expectations from which specific job performance and professional development criteria may be identified. Once these basic criteria have been jointly developed and agreed upon by library media specialists, building principals, and district administrators, they are adopted by the school board.

In addition to basic criteria used for evaluating all library media specialists, individual priority performance indicators are often included in the evaluation. These indicators may change from year to year. They are developed by the library media specialist together with the principal and/or library media director to reflect current program and school needs and objectives.

Responsibility for evaluating building-level library media specialists primarily resides with the principal. Since most principals do not have experience in the library media field as they do in classroom teaching, it is particularly important that the role and function of the library media specialist be clearly defined and jointly agreed upon. District library media directors work cooperatively with the principal to evaluate performance.

The evaluation of support staff for the library media program is based on procedures and instrumentation developed by the district for each personnel classification. Library media specialists participate in the evaluation of nonprofessional personnel who work in the library media program. If the overall responsibility for evaluation resides with other administrators, the library media specialists contribute to the process. All library media program support staff members should have complete and clear job descriptions, systematic assessment of job performance by designated professional staff, and adequate feedback on training and personal development needs.

## Personnel at the District Level

**The importance of providing quality leadership at the district level for library media program development cannot be overstated.** All districts should employ a district library media director to provide leadership and direction to the overall library media program in the district. District supervisors work with library media specialists and building administrators as they develop goals and objectives for their specific programs; provide consultation with library media specialists as they design professional development plans; manage the district-level library media program to support and expand the library media resources at the building level; supervise professional and support staff in the district center; work in partnership with other district-level directors to encourage personnel with whom they work to integrate library media resources and programs into their specific work areas; provide library, media, and information resources and services to district-level educators; and serve as strong advocates to the district administration and community at large for school library media program support.

The district library media director is selected on the basis of knowledge and experience at one or more levels in the library media program and managerial, administrative, and supervisory competencies. The district library media director meets the academic criteria and requirements for building-level library media specialists, as well as for district library media director certification. Furthermore, the district library media director demonstrates competence in planning, evaluating, and managing human resources. Depending on the size and scope of the district program, the director may be expected to have the same administrative and supervisory education and certification as other administrators in curriculum and instructional roles.

A number of factors influence the staff size, staffing pattern, and range of services offered at the district level. Some of these include: the organization, size, and budget of the district; the service expectations both building- and district-level personnel hold for the district library media program; policies related to budget planning and allocation; availability of services from other agencies and programs; and quantity and range of instructional materials and equipment available at the building level. Districts may cooperate with other districts or regional units for certain services (such as centralized processing or access to sophisticated technology) or even personnel as a feasible alternative to establishing their own district-level services. Further discussion of the roles and responsibilities of the district library media director may be found in chapter 8.

## Guidelines for Personnel

Each school, regardless of size or level, has at least one full-time library media specialist who serves full-time as the head of the library media program within the building.

Library media specialists are members of the school's instructional staff and participate fully in the planning, delivery, and evaluation of the school curriculum and of student learning activities.

Library media specialists have master's level education with preparation in library and information science, management, education, media, communications theory, and technology.

The library media staff includes one or more paid technicians, assistants, or clerks for each library media professional.

The number of professional staff needed in any building is determined through an identified planning process, which takes into account program requirements, the number of students and teachers who are served, and other pertinent features of the school and the library media center itself.

Library media personnel are available to teachers and students throughout the school day and do not have their time rigidly scheduled with classes.

Library media specialists are evaluated at the building level through instruments which address their unique responsibilities and contributions according to established district practices for all professional personnel.

Library media staff members have salary, fringe benefits, and working conditions equal to those of other staff members with comparable qualifications and responsibilities.

The head of the library media program is accorded pay, responsibilities, and administrative standing commensurate with other leadership positions in the school and serves on the school's curriculum or instructional body.

Library media specialists engage in continuing education activities to ensure that they are qualified to deliver library media programs that reflect the most recent developments in education, technology, and information science.

Leadership and coordination are provided at the district level by a library media specialist chosen on the basis of educational preparation, breadth of experience, and administrative qualifications.

## Selected Readings

Herrin, Barbara, Louis R. Pointon, and Sara Russell. "Personality and Communications Behaviors of Model School Library Media Specialists." *Drexel Library Quarterly* 21, no. 2 (Spring 1985): 69–90.

Probes the personality characteristics of successful school library media specialists.

Pfister, Fred C. and Nelson Towle. "A Practical Model for a Developmental Appraisal Program for School Library Media Specialists." *School Library Media Quarterly* 11, no. 2 (Winter 1983): 111–121.

Pfister's model as based on research in Florida school districts.

Pfister, Fred C., Joyce P. Vincelette, and Jonnie B. Sprimont. "An Integrated Performance Evaluation and Program Evaluation System: A

Case Study of Pasco County, Florida." *School Library Media Quarterly* 14, no. 2 (Winter 1986): 61–66.

Further research by Pfister produced an evaluation system for the school library media specialist.

Tennessee Career Ladder Better Schools Program. *Library Media Specialist Orientation Manual 1986–87.* Nashville: Tennessee Department of Education, 1986.

An in-depth program for evaluating the performance of the library media specialist. Performance appraisal is based on multiple sources of information and is used for a merit pay system.

# Resources and Equipment

The library media center's resources and equipment serve as the primary information base and the tools through which library media specialists make ideas and information available to students and teachers. The information needs of the school community are met through collections available within the school and through access to information and resources in other locations.

The term *collection* has traditionally signified the information base contained within the school. Today, the collection embraces not only the library media center's instructional materials—print and nonprint (including audio, visual, and electronically stored information)—but also equipment necessary to manage, produce, and use them. All such materials and equipment are considered part of the school library media center collection, regardless of funding source or the area of the school in which they are housed.

Other resources needed for learning today are not part of the collection, which is housed on the school premises. Information may be accessed through electronic means or satellite reception, or borrowed from agencies with which the school has cooperative agreements. The information resources provided in these ways are referred to as "information services."

Two current trends are having significant impact on the traditional library media collection. First, as technological advances provide new ways of recording, packaging, and delivering data, images, and information, the resources available to schools and learners are expanding exponentially. Second, in order to meet the needs of individual students and of changing educational programs, library media resources are being more fully integrated into the overall school curriculum. As a result, developing the collection requires an active partnership among teachers, administrators, and the library media specialist in order to tailor collections and information services to specific school programs. Both of these trends indicate that the information base of tomorrow's school will differ greatly from that of the past.

## Scope of the Collection

Students must have access to a wide range of information resources. Both students and teachers are entitled to collections that provide access to current, representative, and appropriate resources and information that will satisfy their educational needs and interests and match their individual learning styles. Resources that cover all appropriate topics and represent a diversity of points of view are essential.

Library media specialists, working with teachers, administrators, and students, select or produce materials to meet the overall goals of the school and the learning objectives designed by teachers for specific curricula. In addition, materials are needed to enrich and extend the curriculum and to meet the personal information interests of students.

Traditionally, the library media center collection has included fiction and nonfiction books, periodicals, pamphlets, manuscripts, reports, prints, posters, microforms, textbooks (basic and supplementary), workbooks, multimedia packages or kits, specimens, realia, models, audio and video recordings, filmstrips, slides, computer disks, films, locally produced materials, and other book and nonbook materials in various formats.

Collections are now in a state of transition. With the rapid changes and advances in technology, the library media collection includes new formats and delivery systems. Compact discs, CD-ROM, video discs, optical discs, videotex, computer software, interactive video, and cable and satellite transmission all have library media program applications and are now part of library media center collections. Further technological developments are likely to occur, necessitating a continuous evaluation of new information systems for access, production, storage, and delivery in order to assess their potential benefits to teachers and students.

Materials that have been produced locally to meet specific classroom or learner requirements constitute an element in the library media center collection unique to the individual school. Locally produced materials include all forms of print, visual, audio, and electronic resources and are in no way synonymous with duplication of purchased materials. These one-of-a-kind resources— produced by teachers, students, and the library media center staff—are evaluated for potential use by others and added to the collection in the same manner as purchased materials. As technology improves the ease with which high-quality learning resources can be created, this portion of the collection may increase considerably.

In addition to meeting the needs of student users, the library media center collection includes professional materials and information services to help teachers keep abreast of trends, developments, techniques, research, and experimentation in general and specialized educational fields. Materials dealing with student learning and behavior may also be of use to parents and other community members.

The availability of resources outside the school enhances the local collection but does not replace it. Each school, and each school district, must provide the primary resources needed by its students and teachers and must provide those resources at the time of need and at the nearest point of possible use. Although schools will broaden the information resources available to users through direct electronic access, students and teachers will continue to need a well-selected building-level collection capable of satisfying a large percentage of the instructional resource needs.

It may be desirable to develop local information sources and systems. Such databases can include community resource files, which teachers can use to locate experts for class presentations or identify field trip sites, and community service files, which list services and goods available for specific needs.

School library media centers sometimes contain special collections that include such resources as rare or unusual books, historical materials donated by a parent or alumnus, school or community archival materials, and local or student authors' collections. Such collections may be housed separately and circulated according to special school policies. Items of great value and those that are not replaceable may require carefully controlled access. Special collections should be included in the centralized bibliographic record to encourage their use.

Convenience and high usage may dictate that certain library media resources be housed closer to point of use, such as in subject resource centers. All such resources, regardless of location, should be considered as information sources for the entire school and should be available to all users as needed. Centralized automated bibliographic control identifies the location of these materials to facilitate access.

The size of the school's internal holdings remains an important consideration. However, with the transition today to varied formats and more direct delivery of information, establishing a recommended size becomes increasingly difficult. Traditional methods of counting items are inappropriate for many media formats, and volume alone does not assure an adequate number of items to support a particular need. However, in order to provide school library media specialists with some information, statistics on print and other media holdings, arranged by school size and level, are found in Appendix A.

Adequacy of the collection size is best determined through an evaluation of how well the collection and information services are meeting the needs of the users. Criteria that can be applied to assess the adequacy of collection size include: determining whether the collection is large enough to satisfy a certain percentage of requests; whether it represents basic titles and sources recommended in standard selection tools; and whether, as judged by users themselves, it offers sufficient materials to stimulate and promote literacy development and to support special program emphases. An overriding concern must be for the recency of the information contained in the materials. The collection must include works by contemporary authors and producers and meet the interests and needs of today's students.

## Collection Development

Collection development is a systematic process administered by the library media staff to bring together the materials and equipment to meet users' needs. Part of the collection development process today includes consideration of information services as well as the development of a collection housed within the school.

All schools must have a collection development plan that addresses their collection needs and includes such specific steps as school/community analysis, policy development, selection, acquisition, weeding, and evaluation. Some of these steps are also appropriate at the district level, especially the development of a district-wide selection policy.

All formats of information are considered for the collection and are evaluated on the basis of their utility in meeting instructional, informational, and other user needs in the school community. The acquisition of new and innovative modes of information delivery is part of the collection development process. Care must be taken to assure that there is appropriate and sufficient equipment to use each format efficiently and that students and teachers have adequate instruction in its use.

The collection includes materials to meet the needs of all learners, including the gifted, the mentally, physically, and emotionally impaired, and those who are culturally disadvantaged or from linguistic minorities. When the internal holdings do not meet all needs, library media specialists are responsible for making arrangements to secure materials from other sources. Provision must also be made for students who need specific pieces of equipment in order to obtain information; such equipment includes braille writers, adapted electronic and telephone equipment, enlarged print devices and other specialized tools.

Students in remote sites may require specialized access and delivery systems to assure that they, too, have equal access to learning resources. Rotating collections, interlibrary loan, online databases, satellite television and radio broadcast, and computer delivery systems are examples of ways to address the information resource needs of such students.

### District Selection Policy

**All schools within a district must adhere to a common, district-wide selection policy that has been adopted by the Board of Education as official district policy.** A district policy provides general guidelines for the selection of materials and equipment at all schools, and

- establishes the only legal basis for selection and removing materials from the collection
- establishes the objectives for the selection of materials
- identifies responsibilities of personnel who participate in the selection process
- identifies types of materials and equipment to be considered
- states the criteria to be followed in evaluating materials
- defines procedures for selection, for periodic re-evaluation of titles in existing collections, and for handling challenged titles
- includes the process for periodic review and revision of the policy.

The development and implementation of the district-wide selection policy is coordinated by the director of the district library media program or a district official who has been assigned that responsibility. The designated official works cooperatively with representatives of the library media staff, administrators, consultants, teachers, students, and other community members to develop selection policies. Schools without such district leadership should work together to develop a common policy and seek its adoption by the school board.

The following principles help to determine selection objectives: resources are appropriate for the students for whom they are selected; resources represent diverse points of view; resources stimulate growth in analytical and thinking skills; and resources are appropriate to the educational program and school community. These objectives apply to all forms of information: books, pamphlets, periodicals, microforms, databases, computer discs, laser discs, videos, films, and other mediated presentations.

The major criterion used for the selection of resources is the educational suitability of the resource for its intended use. Other criteria include:

1. **intellectual content of the material:** scope, arrangement and organization, relevance and recency of information, special features, and overall value to the collection
2. **philosophy and goals of the school district:** resources support and are consistent with the educational goals of the district and with goals and objectives of individual schools and specific courses

3. **characteristics of the user:** Resources are appropriate for the age, emotional development, ability levels, learning styles, and social development of the students for whom the resources are selected.

The selection policy reflects and supports principles of intellectual freedom described in the Library Bill of Rights (ALA), Freedom to Read (ALA and AAP), Access to Resources and Services in the School Library Media Program: An Interpretation of the Library Bill of Rights (AASL), and the Statement on Intellectual Freedom (AECT). Copies may be found in Appendix D.

Policies outlining the steps for fair, timely, and orderly handling of requests for materials to be reconsidered are important to create the environment needed to support school collections. The complainant's rights and responsibilities are clearly stated, as are the procedures to be followed by the school and the district in the event of a request for reconsideration.

Selection policies cover all resources used in the district, including textbooks and classroom instructional resources, although in some districts, separate policies exist for the selection and re-evaluation of classroom resources and teaching methods. If separate policies are developed, school library media specialists, because of their unique expertise, are in a position to assume a leadership role in the development of policies consistent with those governing the school library media program.

### Collection Development Planning

Collection development planning occurs at the school level and is based upon a needs assessment of the school population. The collection development plan provides a broad overview of the needs and priorities of the school's collection, based on the short- and long-range goals of the library media program and on an assessment of the strengths and weaknesses of the collection, and provides specific guidelines for building and maintaining the school's collection.

The school's collection development plan states the philosophy and goals of the school and the library media program and relates collection decisions to these goals. It defines the users and programs to be served; identifies sources of funds for the collection; establishes priorities, limitations, and categories of materials to be collected or excluded; correlates collection development with the curriculum; defines criteria for weeding and replacement of materials and equipment; and addresses the issue of reproduction of materials. Responsibilities for resource sharing and networking are identified. The plan also identifies who is responsible for selection decisions.

For a school's collection development plan to be effective, it must be developed in cooperation with the teachers and the principal and reviewed by the district media director and curriculum coordinator. A provision for periodic review of the plan is included. At the school level, the collection development process includes the following steps:

1. *School/community analysis.* An understanding of the school community is a critical factor in the collection development process. A systematic assessment by the library media specialists of the information needs of the users to be served is the first step. Data on users' needs can be gathered by examining demographic characteristics and obtained through formal and informal surveys of students, teachers, administrators, and parents. Advice should also come from an advisory committee to the library media program. Such a committee typically includes department heads, subject specialists, parents, students, and school administration, and helps identify characteristics of the school population, the curriculum, and the special programs within the school. Additional information can be gathered by evaluating use patterns.

2. *Selection.* Selection of materials at the school level follows criteria established by the district policy. Identification of specific titles is a joint effort among teachers, the library media staff, and students, and meets needs determined both formally and informally. Direct examination of potential materials is invaluable in the selection process. When it is not possible, published reviews and quality selection tools must be used. Other aids in the selection process include visits to evaluation centers and other libraries and exhibits at conferences.

In selecting information resources for the library media program, both the internal holdings and available information services must be considered so that newer forms of information and technology can be incorporated at the appropriate time and in accordance with curriculum needs. Selection of media, equipment, and communications access and distribution systems must be coordinated. The contributions of resource sharing through networking programs, interlibrary loans, multitype library consortia and resource sharing cooperatives, online searches of databases, and telecommunications delivery of information are also taken into consideration when selecting the media to be added to the school collection.

3. *Acquisition.* Acquisition is the process of securing materials for the library media collection, whether by purchase, gift, rental, or local production. Acquisition procedures identify the appropriate sources for obtaining the material and outline the processes by which the media specialist orders, receives, and pays for the materials.

Acquisition procedures are uniform in the district. Many procedures, such as ordering, record keeping and accounting, are established by an agent for the school district and are frequently automated. In some instances, regional and commercial services are viable alternatives to district-level acquisitions. Whatever system is used, it must be efficient, cost-effective, and provide materials quickly, at the lowest cost, and with the least amount of effort required by the school staff.

The acquisition process includes obtaining a machine-readable record of each item's standard cataloging. Standardization of records is important if school districts are to fully participate in resource-sharing activities. Use of the accepted library standard—the MARC (machine-readable cataloging) record, the Library of Congress number, and ISBN (International Standard Book Number)—will help prepare library media centers for future automation.

4. *Evaluation.* Evaluation of collection plans, of the collection as a whole, and of individual items must be ongoing. Evaluation of the collection relates what exists in the collection to what is needed; provides guidance for making decisions about the collection; provides a measure of the effectiveness of the plan; and directs monetary resources to areas needing attention. Library media specialists use accepted techniques of measurement and evaluation in order to obtain the information required for collection development.

Specific techniques for evaluating the collection include evaluation by subject experts, user satisfaction surveys of teachers and students, analysis of inventory and circulation statistics, and collection mapping, which describes the collection in terms of present strengths and weaknesses.

Considerations in the evaluation process include the following:

Does the collection support and enhance specific courses and units of instruction taught in the schools?

For any unit of instruction is/are there
—a variety of media?
—materials that are current?
—enough materials for the number of users?
—materials that span reading, viewing, listening, and comprehension levels?
—materials that span the opinion/cultural/political spectrum, if required?
—materials of interest to students?

## Organization, Maintenance, and Circulation

### Organization

To assure that resources are readily accessible and available through the library media center, all information resources, regardless of format, are part of a bibliographic control system. Central or commercial processing should be considered for uniformity and to save time for building-level staff; it should be considered for all permanent materials. Users can locate classified and cataloged materials through use of a card, book, or electronic catalog. Other means of bibliographic control are used for materials that are consumable or that are used primarily for browsing. Regardless of what systems are used, the organization of all collections should be logical and attempt to follow standardized procedures.

All schools should actively plan for the automation of their records and procedures. Automated systems provide accurate and efficient ways of circulating and locating materials and enable the library media specialist to work more closely with students and teachers. Automated systems provide useful data regarding the circulation and use of various media, subject areas, and student needs. When developed cooperatively within districts, cities, and regional/state areas, valuable information is readily available to facilitate interlibrary loan and resource sharing. Part of the planning process will include an assessment of the most cost-effective way and the appropriate timeline for the school to convert to automated systems. Careful and sequential planning is most important.

School library media collections now include materials in many different formats that require a variety of storage and housing considerations. Some school library media specialists may choose to physically integrate the print and nonprint materials in order to increase their use. However, the different storage requirements and the "non-browsability" of some media may make the physical integration of all formats difficult. If the collection is not physically integrated, the catalog guides users to the location of resources.

### Maintenance

All collections should be inventoried periodically to assure that the record of the collection actually reflects what is available to the user. Regular inventories also provide valuable information for the selection process. Inventories should not reduce the availability of the collection to students during the regular school calendar; extended employment or additional staff may be required to complete the inventory. Modern automated circulation systems provide fast and accurate ways to inventory collections and to provide statistical information useful to collection building and maintenance.

Data from inventory counts are useful in the process of removing obsolete items from the collection. Having outdated or inaccurate materials in a collection discourages use, gives a false impression of the adequacy of the collection, wastes the time of the staff, and obstructs users in their search for useful materials.

Criteria for removing items are identified in the school's collection development plan and provide guidelines for evaluating physical deterioration, obsolescence, and appropriateness for the current needs of the school community. Duplicate copies, out-of-date materials, materials no longer used or of slight utility, almanacs, yearbooks and encyclopedias that have been superseded by newer editions should be covered in the criteria for removal from the collection. Materials in which any significant portion of the information is outdated are withdrawn. Criteria for replacing equipment and procedures for disposing of outmoded, unused, or irreparable equipment are included in the collection development plan.

Schools with any significant loss of materials should consider the installation of an electronic security system. These systems can reduce losses as well as assure that materials will be available to all students and faculty when needed.

### Circulation

Systems and policies for circulating materials ensure maximum use and encourage students to borrow materials for use throughout the school, at home, and in the library media center. Circulation policies reinforce the concept of free access to library media centers for minors and safeguard the rights of the individual student to privacy and confidentiality regarding choice of materials. Special care must be exercised to assure that an automated circulation system is not used to gather or store information regarding the nature or subject of a user's resource selections. A copy of the AASL policy on confidentiality may be found in Appendix D.

Library media centers have equipment readily available for student and teacher use to support all the formats of media that the school has acquired. In addition, equipment is available for checkout to classrooms and for overnight use. All equipment must be in good working condition and represent recent advances in media equipment technology. Each piece of equipment is checked on a regular basis through ongoing maintenance and repair service.

## Information Access beyond the School

The advent of library networks, resource-sharing plans, and coordinated collection development efforts offer students and teachers the opportunity to access information beyond the school collection. Online searching of databases and union catalogs of district, regional, and state holdings, in all types of libraries and from all kinds of information agencies, make it possible for schools to identify and locate resources.

A network can be defined as a group of organizations linked through a communication mechanism to accomplish a specified goal. Networking is not limited to libraries; it can provide links to wherever materials are organized for dissemination and use. Networks can be found within a school system or a community or at the county, state, national, and international level. In some cases, the formation of a consortia or network can allow the purchase and sharing of resources that no single school or district could afford. Any such cooperative ventures must be based on careful planning and clearly written policies.

School library media centers join in network activities to improve the quality and range of library media and information services for their users. At the same time, schools make significant contributions to networks by sharing their unique collections. Sharing resources may necessitate changing time-honored patterns of circulation control, cataloging, and even organization of materials. Because school library media centers use public funding to purchase materials and equipment, and because they borrow materials from others, library media specialists must be willing to allow access to resources of the media center by the public whenever use by primary clientele is not abridged. Membership in networks means full participation in lending as well as in borrowing.

Successful interlibrary loan practices that facilitate student use include availability of current indexes and efficient delivery systems at reasonable cost. Automated interlibrary loan systems are making it possible to locate and share resources efficiently and economically. As a result, library media programs can coordinate their collection development efforts in infrequently used areas so that subjects are covered in depth by at least one library or information agency in a district or geographical area. The library media center is an effective access point to other libraries—in the district and beyond—that can supply appropriate information resources.

The opportunities to retrieve information directly from outside the library media center, using commercial databases and area-wide online services, are expanding. In some instances, such information services substitute for the purchase or retention of print and on-site materials. In other cases, direct access expands the resources previously available to users. The selection of vendors, instruction of staff and students in the use of databases, budgeting for costs incurred, and the ethical distribution of such information within the school require the development of new policies and procedures. Library media specialists must develop criteria for evaluating the quality of online services—just as they have done for other media—and for judging its cost-effectiveness in light of all information needs.

The school district or regional resource center provides materials and equipment not normally owned by individual schools. Criteria used to develop such collections include: materials too expensive for each school to own; infrequently used resources and equipment; backup equipment to lend while the school's equipment is being repaired; preview and examination materials; and more extensive professional materials. Developing the district collection requires an understanding of the school programs, a knowledge of materials and equipment available in the buildings, and an awareness of the potential of the newer technologies.

---

## Guidelines for Resources and Equipment

### Scope of the Collection

The library media center collection is selected and developed cooperatively by the library media specialist and the faculty to support the school's curriculum and to contribute to the learning goals of teachers and students.

The library media center collection includes instructional resources in a variety of formats with appropriate equipment selected to meet the learning needs of all students.

Information services provide resources from outside the library media center through interlibrary loan and electronic means to extend and expand the local collection.

## Collection Development

The school district has a selection policy that has been approved by the school board and includes criteria and procedures for the selection and reconsideration of resources.

Each school building has its own collection development plan that supplements a district selection policy and provides specific guidelines for developing the school's collection.

Instructional resources are selected according to principles of intellectual freedom, and provide students with access to information that represents diverse points of view in a pluralistic society.

## Organization, Maintenance, and Circulation

All materials are included in a local bibliographic control system and standardized formats for classification and cataloging are followed.

Full automation of library circulation, cataloging, and acquisition functions is being actively planned and implemented.

Collections and equipment are circulated according to procedures that ensure confidentiality of borrower records and promote free and easy access for all students.

## Information Access beyond the School

The library media center provides access to information outside the center through union catalogs, network arrangements, and resource-sharing options.

District and regional level collections are available to support building-level information needs.

The building-level library media center participates in interlibrary loans, as a lender as well as a borrower according to established policies and procedures.

## Selected Readings

Costa, Betty and Marie Costa. *A Micro Handbook for Small Libraries and Media Centers.* 2nd ed. Littleton, Colo.: Libraries Unlimited, 1986.

The most popular introductory work concerning the use of computers in the school library media program.

Loertscher, David V. and May Lein Ho. *Computerized Collection Development for School Library Media Centers.* Fayetteville, Ark.: Hi Willow Research and Publishing, 1986.

Based on extensive research, this method of collection building matches the collection in a school with curricular targets.

Miller, Marilyn L. and Barbara Moran. "Expenditures for Resources in School Library Media Centers FY '85–'86." *School Library Journal* 33, no. 10 (June–July 1987): 37–45.

Murray, William, ed. *A Guide to Basic Media Materials and Equipment Operations Training.* Aurora, Colo.: Aurora Public Schools, 1985.

An excellent handbook and training guide for simple repair and maintenance of audiovisual equipment.

White, Brenda H., ed. *Collection Management for School Library Media Centers.* New York: Hayworth Press, 1986. (Also published as *Collection Management,* vol. 7, no. 3/4 (Fall, 1985/Winter 1985–1986.)

A collection of theoretical and practical articles written by many well-known library media specialists and library educators.

Woolls, E. Blanche and David V. Loertscher. *The Microcomputer Facility and the School Library Media Specialist.* Chicago: American Library Association, 1986.

A collection of original articles from practitioners concerning the management of the microcomputer as part of both teaching and administrative functions.

# Facilities

Library media center facilities within a district or a school provide the space for the materials, equipment and services, needed to achieve the mission, goals, and objectives of the library media program. Since differences exist in the goals and patterns of educational programs, facilities within the school are designed to reflect its curriculum and the particular instructional requirements of its students and teachers. The size and characteristics of school populations and the rapidly changing technologies for instruction demand alternatives and maximum flexibility in the design and relationship of functional spaces within the library media program facilities.

## The Planning Process

When a decision is made to remodel a present facility or construct a new building or library media center, the library media staff should take part from the beginning in all aspects of the planning. In situations in which new schools are being added to the district, the planning team will include the district library media director as well as building-level library media specialists selected from the school's future staff or from other buildings. (In the latter case, the building-level representatives will act as advisors to the district-level personnel who are responsible for the new building.) It is highly advisable to bring in consultants experienced in the design and development of library media facilities. Such specialized help should be sought early in the planning process; it can save considerable time and money and help produce a more attractive and functional facility.

Library media staff must be actively engaged in the entire planning process, working with teachers and administrators to determine how the library media facility will relate to the overall school program. Library media specialists must prepare adequately for the planning process. Participation in planning demands a general understanding of the process itself, from preliminary planning through final construction. A familiarity with architectural terms and concepts is a prerequisite.

Planning for library media facilities should begin as soon as the decision is made to construct, expand, or renovate a facility. Library media specialists involved in the project must assume leadership in the planning process and be actively involved in the decision-making aspects of the project. The steps in the planning process are as follows:

1. The initial phase entails evaluating the existing or proposed library media program with respect to the school's educational goals and objectives.
2. Future needs of the library media program must be considered, including those new technologies that have potential for changing the delivery and use of information and ideas. Projections of future needs are based on the recognition that the library media program is an integral part of the instructional program and, as such, functions as an extension of every classroom.
3. The data generated from the evaluation and projections must be translated into a written plan that incorporates the basic guidelines suggested by the library media profession and adheres to the guidelines of the school system and state agencies. The plan should include a statement of the philosophy, goals, and objectives of the library media program in relation to school and district philosophy and goals. It may also include a statement that defines the library media center's physical orientation within the building itself.
4. A more detailed written statement of educational specifications defining each space within the library media facility is generally required by the architect. Included for

each space will be the name of the space, the desired size of the space, the number of occupants who will use the space, and a description of its function. Typically, this description will include the relationship of the space to other areas within the library media center and within the larger context of the building. It will also include any special environmental and furnishing considerations, a list of fixed and movable equipment, and any other pertinent information.

5. Throughout the planning process, constant monitoring by the building-level library media specialist, the district library media director, and the building principal is necessary to assure that program needs are well understood by architect and builder. All major decisions must be adequately discussed by all relevant parties including the library media specialists and have the approval of the board of education and district administrators. Revisions made without input from the library media program representatives can seriously affect the quality of the library media facility.

## Library Media Facilities in the School

A plan for school library media program facilities carefully interprets the program functions and determines the spaces required for those functions. The arrangement of facilities should create an environment that encourages the use of various media, facilitates inquiry, helps motivate students to use the materials and services necessary for learning, and provides the design flexibility needed to accommodate new technologies.

### Functions and Spaces

#### Access to Information

The central function of the library media center facility is the housing, circulation, and centralized distribution of the collection of information resources and equipment used in the school's instructional program. It is here that learning resources are acquired and made available for use, necessitating space for ordering, processing, and storage. The facility also includes spaces for primary activities such as displaying indexes, reference tools, and special collections, circulating general materials, housing the collection for user access, and providing equipment for using all types of media.

Because interaction between students and the library media staff is important for accessing information and for reference services, space must be carefully arranged to encourage such assistance. The library media facility may include provision for all instructional materials, including textbooks, or it may be limited to the centralized collection, with storage and checkout of classroom texts handled elsewhere. Increasingly, space is needed for the equipment and resources used to identify and access information outside the library media center and the school and for electronic distribution of media.

### Teaching and Learning

The library media facility provides students and teachers with adequate resources and spaces to be used for learning in all aspects of the school's curriculum. Facilities are required that encourage the student to study independently, to interact and work cooperatively with other students in both small and large group settings, and to receive formal and informal instruction from teachers and the library media specialist. Facilities and equipment must also be available to encourage and support the production and communication of ideas and information in a variety of media and formats. The school library media center must present a welcoming and inviting atmosphere if it is to foster learning for all students and teachers.

### Consulting and Planning

The library media program facilities must provide space for teachers to engage in curriculum development and in the planning of instructional activities. Such planning requires places to select, review, produce, or use materials needed to meet specified goals. It requires proximity to the media collection and ready access to production facilities. The library media specialist and the teacher need spaces in which to work together to carry out instructional design processes.

## Design and Relationships

The interrelationship of the library media center to the instructional program must be the guiding principle in the design and placement of the facility within the school. Appearance and aesthetics are also important. The library media center should be pleasing and inviting to users, reflecting knowledge of how spaces, arrangements, acoustics, and furnishings affect student behavior. The goal is to make the facilities as accessible and welcoming as possible, in order to encourage staff and student use.

The library media center should be near the classrooms and easily accessible to students and teachers throughout the school day. Locating the center close to study areas facilitates frequent use and minimizes time lost in transit. When the auditorium, theater, and large group areas are nearby and easily accessible, projection and recording equipment can be moved in and out quickly and efficiently.

Although limited in number for security purposes, access points should be conveniently located near classrooms and outside entrances. The library media center should have its own outside entrance so that full library media services can be offered beyond the regular school schedule.

It is important to work with the architect to plan for a suitable relationship among all functional areas in the center, recognizing the importance of the relationship of media center spaces to outside corridors and to other spaces within the school building. The schematic plan shown in figure 1 is an example of how such spaces can relate to one another.

Planners are urged to consult texts and articles depicting a variety of spatial relationships to help determine a workable design. Considerations include:

- assuring that the plans take into account the typical traffic flow of individuals and groups in and out of the center and within the center
- relating the spaces for supporting activities to the spaces for users' services
- establishing good visibility among all parts of the center where supervision is necessary
- recognizing the natural flow from indexes to the collection for retrieval of desired materials and equipment, and to areas where materials and equipment are used

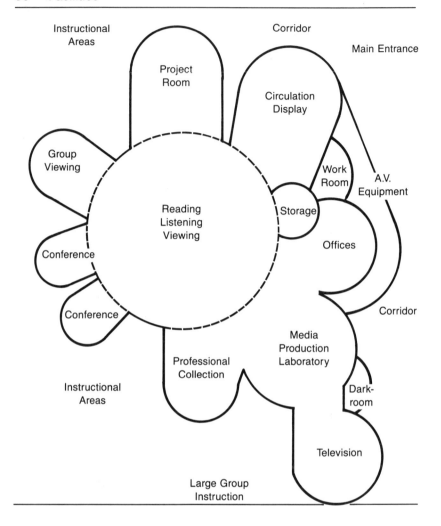

Figure 1. Schematic representation of spaces by location

- realistically assessing security needs, including material or book detection systems, with particular regard to the increasing amount of expensive, attractive, and popular electronic equipment housed in the media center
- providing barrier-free routes for physically impaired patrons, with particular attention to bookstack areas, catalog and circulation areas, and seating spaces.

Safety considerations are of critical importance and include securely fastened equipment, an emergency power shut-off; solidly built stations and storage units, smooth floors, and use of safety glass. For fire prevention and fire preparedness, exits must be clearly marked, doors must be equipped with crash bars, fire extinguishers must be available, and a written evacuation plan must be posted in key locations.

The increasing use of audiovisual and electronic media, both in the delivery of instruction and in accessing different information sources, requires new design considerations. Significant attention must be directed at control of lighting and room-darkening design. Increased use of equipment requires adequate and flexible electrical outlets and provision for future cabling, communications systems, and electronic delivery within the building from the library media center. Static electricity reduction, air conditioning, and humidity requirements must be considered.

These and many other design and arrangement factors must be considered as new and remodeled facilities are planned to assure that the space will be both functional and flexible. The importance of flexibility of design cannot be overemphasized.

## Spaces and Arrangements

Among the specific variables to be considered in the design of facilities are the differences between elementary and secondary schools, the differences in school populations and community involvement, the total amount of space available, and the extent of centralized district services. Both the present situation and future technological changes must be taken into account in analyzing these variables. The following specifications should be incorporated into planning or reviewing library media program facilities at the building level:

1.  Reading, listening, viewing, and computing areas for independent study, with ready access to collections and equipment. Considerations include:

    a.  individual study spaces provided by carrels or study tables

    b.  tables, counters, carrels, or carts to accommodate a variety of electronic equipment

    c. informal seating or an informal area with comfortable chairs

    d. special carrels and equipment for users with physical or sensory impairments.

2. Space for small and medium-sized group activities, either as conference rooms or as specially organized and acoustically treated areas within the general seating space, for viewing, discussing, and working on projects. Considerations include:

    a. in elementary school library media centers, the incorporation of a storytelling area equipped for dramatizations and electronic presentations

    b. adequate space and appropriate furnishings for small group work with newer technologies, such as computers and interactive video.

3. A large multipurpose area off the main area of the library media center, serving as a viewing room, lecture hall, classroom, or meeting area. Considerations include:

    a. a control room to provide special lighting and sound

b. convenient access to audiovisual equipment and technical support

c. movable seating to provide flexibility

d. floor coverings appropriate to multipurpose activities.

4. Space to house and display the collections of library media materials, provide a supervised entry-exit area, organize reference materials and index tools for easy access, and carry out circulation and reserve activities. Considerations include:

a. the changing nature of collections, such as the increased packaging of information in electronic or audiovisual formats, the storage of periodicals on microfiche or microfilm instead of paper copy, the distribution of films on videocassettes, and the acquisition of computer discs and other software

b. the need for electronic access to information within and outside the center through online services, CD-ROM capability, and computerized catalogs

c. dedicated telephone and data lines for access to information sources and television outside the school building

d. space for the storage of hard copy made from electronic sources and the copy equipment to transfer information from nonprint to print media

e. the space required for physical access to and control or distribution of special technologies, such as CD-ROM, optical laser discs, hard disks, satellite systems, magnetic storage, electronic distribution systems, and other emerging technologies

f. space and raceways to allow use of electrical and electronic technologies for security systems, automated circulation systems, and computerized catalogs

g. well-placed and secure space for displays and promotional materials

h. fireproof space with compact shelving and adequate theft protection for storage of archives and important school records.

5. Facilities for the organization, maintenance, and control of equipment in the center, for the preparation and maintenance of all materials in the collection, for the production of materials by teachers, students, production specialist, and staff, and for the delivery of information within the school. Considerations include:

   a. areas for consultation with teachers and students
   b. work areas where library media personnel carry out technical processes and support activities
   c. facilities for the production of materials, including graphics, photography, videotaping, audio production, computer programming
   d. a secure equipment area from which distribution, repair, and maintenance of equipment can be carried out, with convenient access to hallway, elevator, loading dock
   e. spaces where students and teachers have ready access to equipment to view, listen, read, and compute, using media in all formats
   f. space for the distribution systems, which capture and rebroadcast instructional television, radio, computer programs, and audio and video teleconferencing or distance learning.

6. Facilities for computers for both administrative and teaching or learning applications, within the library media center. Space requirements vary with the nature of computer use and its relation to the school program. Considerations include:

   a. the number of computer laboratories in the building and the nature of their use
   b. the flexibility demanded by services such as database searching, dial access, computerized catalog, automated circulation systems, interactive video
   c. the relationship of the library media center to other learning areas, such as distance learning labs and satellite resource centers.

7. Space where faculty and media professionals can work without student interruption, where professional materials can be housed and displayed, and where general purpose

equipment, such as typewriters, computers, and copiers, is available for teacher use.

## Equipment and Furnishings

Equipment and furniture are chosen for their usefulness and appropriateness. Selections are based on knowledge of the educational program of the school, the size of the collection, the formats to be housed and accessed, the age and size of the students, community expectations, and the future needs of the library media program.

When selecting furniture and equipment, consider the following criteria:

1. Adjustable shelves of a standard size and height are used throughout the center, including special units for large reference works, picture books, and quarto books. Storage units for materials in microform and other audiovisual and electronic formats are versatile and provide convenient access as well as protection for the media.
2. Chairs must be comfortable, sturdy, and attractive.

3. Furniture must be the right size and height for the students who will use it; special pieces should be purchased as necessary for the disabled and others with special needs.
4. Furnishings and equipment are durable and easy to maintain.
5. Quality furnishings and industrial grade equipment are recommended as cost-effective for the heavy use which is normal in a school setting.

## District Library Media Facilities

Facilities for a district media program are designed to support the educational goals of the schools in the district and to enhance and augment the building-level library media programs. In order to provide maximum convenience for access, use, communication, and administration, the facilities for the district library media program should be in the school district administrative center. Assignment of space should give priority to library media program administration, to the professional materials collection, to conference areas, and to the library media selection and evaluation center. These program elements can then be readily accessible to curriculum specialists, to other administrators, to special committees, and to other school personnel. Functions at the district or regional level include: technical processing of all materials, including textbooks; equipment repair and maintenance; printing and graphics services; film and video library collections; television distribution; media production; facilities for origination of distance learning; and facilities for examination of materials, including computer software.

### Spaces and Relationships

The requirements for a district library media facility are as follows:

1. An area for planning and administration of the district library media program, including necessary office space, close to curriculum specialists
2. Conference rooms, meeting rooms, and demonstration areas as needed to facilitate staff developments and to pro-

vide consultative services in curriculum development and instructional design

3. A professional library and teacher center where all types of professional materials and equipment can be housed to accommodate reading, study, listening, and viewing of those materials by faculty and staff

4. A separate area for the selection and evaluation of library media materials and equipment, both for individual and group viewing

5. Space to house a collection of district materials that supplements the building collections. This area may be part of the professional library or may be located adjacent to the processing center

6. An equipment services area, large enough to provide for selection, evaluation, inspection, repair, maintenance, distribution, and storage of new and old equipment, with adequate space for efficient work flow for technicians and clerical workers

7. A processing center where materials, equipment, and supplies can be received, processed, cataloged, and distributed. This area requires space for office workers, arrangement for efficient work flow, and provision for adequate storage. Easy access to an outside entry and an elevator for shipping and receiving is essential.

8. Production areas, both electronic and other, as required by the instructional program of the district and as needed to supplement the building level programs. Sufficient space must be provided in each to carry out the required functions while providing space for production specialists to plan and work.

Provision must be made for areas where production specialists can confer with instructional and curriculum specialists. Careful consideration must be given to the impact of new and emerging technologies in the production field, especially the interaction of such devices as computers and television and the demands this may have on facilities. Production spaces include:

a. graphics, photography, and printing—requires consideration of space for production of art work and printed materials, for production and reproduction equipment, for

printing equipment, for paper storage located near ma-
chines, for refrigeration equipment for photographic and
other supplies, and for an air-conditioned darkroom with
light locks and warning system.

b.  audiotape production—requires space for recorders and
duplicators and control of sound reverberation. Combin-
ing this area with a television production studio control
room may be feasible.

c.  radio studio—requires recording studio and control booth
for live production with adequate sound control. It may be
feasible to combine this with other areas in production
services.

d.  television production—requires consideration of the extent to which television production facilities are used at individual school building sites, the contracting of
television production, the use of programming by other
existing agencies, the use of portable mini-studios and
portable videotape units, the district's involvement in two-
way television, and the emergence of interactive video
technology.

## Guidelines for Facilities

### School Building Facilities

Facilities provide a barrier-free learning environment and unimpeded physical access for all users.

Facilities have built-in flexibility, so that changing needs and newer information-handling technologies can be accommodated in the existing complex without extensive redesign.

Facilities are located to provide easy access and encourage frequent use, allowing for traffic flow that minimizes interruptions and distractions.

Facilities have a separate outside entrance and are located to make them readily accessible before, during, and after school hours and during vacation periods.

Facilities provide a comfortable, efficient, and safe working environment for students, teachers, administrators, and library media staff.

Facilities include adequate space for independent study, small and large group activities, reference service, manual and electronic access to the collection, circulation activities, and informal or recreational reading.

Facilities have sufficient space to carry out the support functions (administrative, technical, and consultant) required in providing materials and services.

Facilities have sufficient space for housing materials and the equipment required in production, for evaluation activities, and for the use of such materials and equipment.

Facilities are functional in design and arrangement, aesthetically pleasing in appearance, convenient and comfortable to use.

Facilities have the requisite natural and artificial lighting, acoustical treatment, and climate control for the comfort of the user and for the preservation of materials and equipment.

Facilities are designed to provide the necessary electrical power, light control, circuit surge, telephone and intercommunication devices, sound control, lightning protection, and electronic capabilities required to meet the needs of a changing technological environment.

Facilities are designed with attention to safety precautions such as fire preparedness, emergency exits, securely fastened equipment, and other safeguards that will minimize risk to students, faculty, and staff.

Facilities provide for the unobtrusive security of materials and equipment during the school day and utilize additional electronic and other security measures during non-use hours.

The size of the overall library media center and its spaces, and the relationship of those spaces to each other, help determine the number of library media staff needed to manage and supervise the center.

### District Library Media Facilities

Functions and services are planned in relation to district goals and building-level programs.

Library media personnel assigned to district library media facilities have adequate working space, sufficient equipment, and a pleasing environment.

The quantitative data that accompany these guidelines are presented in Appendix C to help in the planning of functional areas. While quantitative guidelines provide a measure of support for planning, the final decisions for space and areas must be made in light of the requirements of the educational program of the individual district or the school. Planners should note the importance of the general guidelines in evaluating the data, keeping in mind that flexibility in assignment of spaces is essential and that serious consideration should be given to multipurpose use of spaces whenever feasible.

## Selected Readings

Hannigan, Jane A. "Charette: Media Facilities Design." *School Media Quarterly* 2, no. 3 (Spring 1974): 185–294.
    Articles by 20 contributors that cover a wide spectrum of facilities design problems.

Lamkin, Bernice. "A Media Center for the 21st Century." *School Library Journal* 33, no. 3 (November 1986): 25–29.

Lamkin provides a description of the total process of building a new high school library media center from architectural plans through establishing a program in the facility.

*Media Center Facility Design for Maryland Schools.* Baltimore: Maryland State Department of Education, Division of Library Development and Services, 1975. (ERIC# ED 107 297)

# District, Regional, and State Leadership

The function of district, regional, and state library media programs is to support school library media programs. Building-level programs are becoming more dependent upon the support and cooperation of these agencies as information continues to multiply and new developments in technology occur. Schools look to district programs to provide advocacy, some technical services, and opportunities for resource sharing and cooperative programs. The district, in turn, looks to regional and state agencies for leadership in meeting the challenges of automation and change. These partnerships have contributed to the growth and development of school library media programs in the past and promise an even greater degree of institutional cooperation in the future.

Resource sharing—through networking systems, interlibrary loans, telecommunications, and distance learning sites—provides access to information and ideas not available in the school library media center. Cooperative programs at all levels further the principle of equal access to materials and assure the variety of resources needed to meet the individual learning needs of students.

## District Library Media Programs

All school systems must employ a district library media director to provide leadership and direction to the overall library media program. The district director is a member of the administrative staff and serves on committees that determine the criteria and policies for the district's curriculum and instructional programs. The director communicates the goals and needs of both the school and district library media programs to the superintendent, board of education, other district-level personnel, and the community. In this advocacy role, the district library media director advances the concept of the school library media specialist as a partner with teachers and promotes a staffing level that allows the partnership to flourish.

The district library media director is responsible for all aspects of the district program, including personnel, services, facilities, materials, equipment, and operation of centralized services. The director's responsibility for developing a district collection requires a clear understanding of each member school's educational plan and library media program, a knowledge of the materials and equipment in the individual schools, and the needs of new programs in the curriculum.

The director is the liaison for library media-related matters among the schools, the district organization, and the board of education. To perform the role effectively, the library media director must be a specialist in the library media field, knowledgeable about new technology and skillful in the practice of supervision and management.

## Guidelines for District-Level Library Media Personnel

The principal functions that the district library media director performs include the following.

### Leadership

Develops an effective plan and process for providing library media programs that support the philosophy, goals, and objectives of the school district.

Provides leadership and guidance to the school library media staff in program planning, curriculum development, budgeting, inservice activities, facility use, and media production.

Participates in curriculum development, facility planning, personnel staffing, budget and management committees, and task forces and teams at the administrative level.

Articulates a code of ethics that promotes adherence to copyright guidelines.

Advocates the principles of intellectual freedom that govern the universal right to read and to access information and ideas.

Encourages use of new technologies to support teaching and learning.

Directs the district's participation in library networking.

Serves as liaison with supervisory and administrative personnel at local, state, and national levels.

Fosters the development of exemplary library media programs at each educational level and assists the programs in meeting regional, state, and professional standards.

Provides district inservice programs for library media specialists to foster leadership, competence, and creativity in developing programs.

Assists principals, library media specialists, and others in applying district policies that relate to library media programs.

Participates actively in state and national professional associations and encourages a high level of participation by other district media personnel and by building-level personnel.


## Consultation

Assists school library media specialists in developing program goals and objectives.

Promotes expansion of programs that integrate the teaching of skills for finding, evaluating, and using information with the teaching of subject content.

Demonstrates methods for effective integration of library media activities and instructional units in building-level programs.

Consults with planning committees and architects when new or remodeled facilities are designed.

### Communication

Advises district and school administrators of new developments in library media programs, technology, instructional strategies, and research.

Conducts orientation meetings on the library media program for teachers, administrators, and support staff.

Provides building-level library media specialists with information regarding computer-based applications for circulation procedures and public access catalogs.

Develops and implements plans for presenting and publicizing library media programs and services.

Prepares reports for district and school administrators on the impact of building-level programs on the instructional process.

Submits reports to the local board of education, to state and national agencies, to the library media staff, and to the public.

### Coordination

Designs, in coordination with district and building-level instructional leaders, a sequential information skills curriculum to be integrated with classroom teaching activities.

Participates in curriculum development and implementation through membership on instructional, curriculum, textbook, and new program adoption committees.

Coordinates the planning and development of K–12 library media programs that serve the students and staff within the schools.

Coordinates the acquisition and circulation of specialized collections that enrich the curriculum for all grade levels.

### Administration

Works with the principal in selecting and evaluating library media personnel.

Works with the principal to ensure that the library media program furthers the instructional process.

Assists the school library media specialists and principals in developing building-level library media budgets.

Develops the district library media budget, including any allocation for each school, in cooperation with the building principals and library media specialists.

Interprets the library media program and associated budgets for the appropriate administrators.

Furnishes a wide range of resources and services to the school library media program and classroom, e.g., film/video library, production services, television studio, printing services, computer-assisted instruction, and loan of expensive or infrequently used materials or equipment.

Distributes preview and on-approval materials for evaluation/ purchase.

Monitors state and federal laws pertaining to school library media programs.

Monitors the adequacy of collections and equipment to provide data on relevance and currency.

Arranges for building-level library media specialists to evaluate new resources and electronic equipment.

Negotiates contracts and supervises purchase and installation of all resources.

Manages technical services for acquiring and processing resources and for maintaining and circulating district-owned materials and equipment.

Encourages teachers, administrators, and parents to visit library media programs within and outside the district.

Monitors and publicizes the status of district compliance with regional, state, and national accreditation requirements and library media standards.

Provides a professional library collection as well as media and information services for educators.

Seeks and administers grants from federal, state, and regional agencies and from foundations.

Evaluates the impact of library media programs at the district and school levels.

## Regional Library Media Programs

Regional library media programs provide additional services and resources to schools and districts. Regional programs vary in structure, purpose, and services, depending on their functions and scope. The number of regional centers has grown in response to the need for specialized educational services. Regional consortia offer opportunities for evaluation and selection of computer software; access to databases; instructional video courseware and delivery; interactive video development and assessment; and the direct delivery of instruction via satellite.

In some states, a regional program functions as an agent of the state library or the state education agency. In other states, local school districts have cooperated to form and fund a consortium. Other cooperative programs have been created by state legislatures. Funding sources for these centers or programs vary. Units that function as agencies of state programs may be funded by the state legislature. Units developed by cooperating districts are supported by the members through the use of local, state and/or federal funds and by a membership fee structure.

The director of a regional agency or the library media consultant working within a regional agency must be a manager, leader, and consultant. This individual must have comprehensive knowledge of the library media field, be familiar with the curriculum in each district within the region, be alert to services that are needed, and be an astute fiscal manager.

---

### Guidelines for Regional-Level Library Media Personnel

Many services provided by regional library media programs are similar to those provided by district-level library media programs; therefore, only those not commonly provided at other levels are listed below.

#### Leadership

Offers staff development programs for library media specialists, teachers, and administrators.

Provides leadership in evaluating the impact of new and existing technologies and program features.

Promotes the adoption of new and tested technologies in the region, and sets up pilot programs to test new technologies.

Plans for the installation of telecommunication services such as distance learning and teleconferencing.

Participates actively in state and national professional associations, and encourages a high level of participation by district and school library media personnel.

### Consultation

Recommends and encourages visits to exemplary library media programs.

Assists school library media centers in public relations activities.

### Communication

Develops publications, newsletters, videos, and other types of communications for dissemination to the schools.

Alerts schools to legislative initiatives that pertain to or affect school library media programs, curriculum change, graduation requirements, or other matters of interest to educators.

### Coordination

Coordinates school library media program participation in multi-type networks.

Coordinates cooperative preview and purchasing of library media resources and equipment, cooperative bidding, state contracts, and licensing agreements.

### Administration

Produces or distributes instructional television programs, specialized video, film, or other media.

Furnishes technical processing services and access to national bibliographic utilities.

Negotiates rights for distribution, purchase, and rental/lease of media resources to save money through cooperative acquisition and to ensure legal compliance with copyright considerations.

Establishes a preview and examination center for instructional materials and the emerging technologies.

Establishes and oversees a networking system for member schools, including resource sharing, databases, telecommunications, cooperative collection development agreements, cooperative staff, and curriculum development.

Makes available computer and database services for administration and instruction.

Develops specialized collections as appropriate.

Provides and arranges maintenance of audiovisual and computer equipment owned by member schools.

Provides offset printing services, delivery services, media production, and distribution service.

## State Library Media Programs

Variations exist in the organization and responsibilities of state-level library media personnel. Each state board of education establishes policies governing library media programs, certifies personnel to staff library media centers, and may allocate funds for purchase of materials and equipment. Some states have a division of library media personnel within the state education department. In other states, personnel within the state library oversee school library media program development.

All states must have a qualified staff dedicated specifically to school library media programs. Individuals serving in a state-level capacity must be knowledgeable in all phases of library media service, have good human relations skills, and keep informed of current developments in the field and with emerging technologies. These individuals must exert leadership in advocating library media programs and assuring competent professional staffing in library media centers. In all instances, state-level personnel encourage program adherence to state and regional standards and national guidelines.

## Guidelines for State-Level Library Media Personnel

The state agency or designated library media staff assumes responsibility for the functions listed below.

### Leadership

Promotes exemplary professional practices and programs at regional, district, and school levels.

Participates in developing state standards and/or guidelines for library media programs and criteria for certification of library media personnel.

Develops plans for state-based research on library media programs and seeks funding for such research.

Seeks legislative initiatives in support of school library media programs.

Assures that state mandates concerning library media programs are met.

Clarifies certification issues, including evaluation of library and media education programs, and participates in curricular development of these programs.

Participates actively in state and national professional associations, and encourages a high level of participation by district, regional, and school library media personnel.

### Consultation

Provides staff development programs on philosophy, concepts, and trends of library media programs to administrators, supervisors, library media specialists, curriculum directors, and teachers.

Offers consultative services to districts concerning new technologies and services and the planning of media facilities.

Guides districts and regions in the implementation of state policies, laws, and regulations.

Assists schools, districts, and regions in dealing with such problems as censorship challenges.

Participates in the development of state curricular materials.

Reviews library media education programs for approved program status.

## Communication

Collects data and disseminates information on library media programs in the state.

Promotes library media programs through public relations activities.

Receives and disseminates information from state and federal reports related to school library media programs.

Generates publications to assist district- and building-level personnel in providing improved services.

## Coordination

Encourages use of interlibrary loan and cooperative agreements among school, public, academic, and other libraries.

Works cooperatively with state library media associations.

## Administration

Interprets and implements the policies of the state board of education as well as state and federal laws and regulations relating to media in the educational program.

Evaluates library media programs in schools or districts and makes recommendations for their improvement.

Supervises the development of long-range plans for development of effective library media programs.

Makes budget recommendations based on needs assessment for consideration by the appropriate state agency.

Develops guidelines for administration of federal and state funds.

Performs the clearinghouse function for information about state school library media services.

Plans state television programs, services, and networks where appropriate.

State, regional, and district partnerships provide critical support for library media programs at the building level. These partners have varying and complementary responsibilities. All, however, share in the responsibility to provide adequate resources and programs to every user.

# Survey of School Library Media Centers

The Center for Education Statistics of the U.S. Department of Education conducted the most recent survey of school library media programs in 1985 and 1986.* The survey forms were mailed to a nationally representative sample of 4,500 public schools in the fall of 1985 and to 1,700 private schools in January 1986. Data collection continued throughout the 1985–86 school year, and by the end of the study, a response rate of 92 percent for public schools and 86 percent for private schools had been attained. This survey presents the most complete and current picture of school library media programs nationally.

The survey included the kind of data collected in past surveys on growth, numbers of staff, expenditures, facilities, and collections. In addition, for the first time, the survey collected information on the services and technology provided by school library media programs and the uses made of these services. Descriptions of 22 different services that might be offered by library media center staff were included. (These services are listed at the end of this appendix.) Respondents were asked to state how frequently they provide each service— routinely, occasionally, or not at all. Services ranged from traditional ones, such as assisting students in locating information and resources and providing reference assistance to teachers, to newer ones involving video production and cable television.

---

*Center for Education Statistics. Office of Educational Research and Improvement. U.S. Department of Education. *Statistics of Public and Private School Library Media Centers, 1985–86.* Superintendent of Documents, U.S. Government Printing Office, 1987.

## Use of Survey Data in Guidelines

The Office of Educational Research and Improvement of the U.S. Department of Education made the computer tapes containing the survey data available so that the data could be reanalyzed for inclusion in the new guidelines. The analysis was planned and conducted by Dr. Howard D. White (Drexel University) with the advice of Dr. Jacqueline Mancall (Drexel University) and Dr. Roger Tipling (Southwest Missouri State University), and in consultation with the chairperson of the Standards Writing Committee.

Several points should be made about the sample of schools from which data are reported and the way that the tables were constructed:

1. The analysis for the guidelines is based solely on data from the public school sample. (The tape and codebook for the private school sample were received too late to be included.)

2. The public school sample comprises 3,839 schools overall. Of these, 312 were excluded from the analysis as "non-typical." Of these, 284 were "combination" schools (elementary and middle grades combined); the rest were alternative schools, vocational or technical schools, and schools providing special education to the handicapped.

3. In order to determine the high-service programs, each school in the remaining sample of 3,527 was given a score on the basis of how many of the 22 services it occasionally or routinely performed. A 2 was assigned for a service routinely performed, a 1 for service occasionally performed, and a 0 for a service never performed. A school could therefore have a score ranging from 0, if none of the services was performed, to 44, if all the services were routinely performed. Programs scoring 32 and above (that is, one standard deviation above the mean of 23.6) were identified as high-service programs. The library media center programs of 571 schools met the criteria for being designated high-service. All the figures in the guidelines are drawn from this national subsample of 571. The subsample is further broken down by school level and student body size, as follows:

| | |
|---|---:|
| Elementary schools under 500 | 158 |
| Elementary schools over 500 | 114 |
| Middle/junior high schools under 500 | 35 |
| Middle/junior high schools over 500 | 96 |
| High schools under 500 | 32 |
| High schools between 500 and 1,000 | 38 |
| High schools over 1,000 | 98 |
| | 571 |

4. Characteristics regarding staff, budget, collection, microcomputers, and facilities are reported for these programs in three columns. Column 1 provides the levels for schools at the 75th percentile (i.e., 75 percent of the schools in the subsample provide support at this level or lower). Column 2 shows the 90th percentile and Column 3 at the 95th percentile. Thus, in the chart for High Service Programs in Elementary Schools with Under 500 Students, for the variable FTE Total Paid Staff (Professional and Nonprofessional), the 75th percentile is 1.5 (or one and one-half persons) and both the 90th and 95th percentiles are 2.0 (or two full-time persons). The data for each category were calculated independently; therefore, the totals for total FTE paid staff do not equal the sums of the categories listed above.

The collection data are counts. For example, in the same chart, the approximate number of volumes held by High Service Elementary Schools with Under 500 Students is 9,227 volumes by schools at the 75th percentile; 11,117 volumes by schools at the 90th percentile; and 12,809 volumes by schools at the 95th percentile.

Values of all variables within the Budget section should be read as dollars and cents figures. For example, Book Budget per Pupil should be read as $7.74 at the 75th percentile; $11.49 at the 90th percentile; and $16.73 at the 95th percentile. Total figures in budget categories are not cumulative.

The guidelines for library media programs presented throughout INFORMATION POWER are essentially *qualitative* and are intended to provide assistance in striving for excellence. Quantitative descriptions are limited in value because the quantitative characteristics of programs vary in relation to needs and program activities. They are, by no means, the sole criteria by which individual programs should be evaluated. Quantitative descriptions of high quality or "state-of-the-art" programs are included here so that individual school library media specialists may compare their program resources and activities with those of schools identified as high-service providers. The use of level and size categories allows individual readers to select the types and sizes of programs most like their own and to compare their own statistics on facilities, collections, etc., with those of such programs.

Because the national guidelines are intended to provide assistance in striving for excellence, the tables show only the characteristics of programs that deliver high levels of service and not the whole range of current practice. The full report is available from the Department of Education for individuals interested in reviewing the characteristics of programs providing other levels of service.

The following are the 22 services included in the survey:

1. Offers a sequential program of library skills instruction.
2. Coordinates library skills instruction with classroom instruction.
3. Informally instructs students in the use of various types of materials and equipment.
4. Conducts inservice education for teachers in the effective evaluation, selection, and use of media.
5. Assists curriculum committee in selecting appropriate materials and media program activities for resource units and curriculum guides.
6. Helps individual teachers to coordinate media program activities and resources with subject areas, units, and textbooks.
7. Helps teachers to develop, select, implement, and evaluate learning activities requiring various types of media.
8. Provides teachers with information about new educational and media developments.
9. Provides reference assistance to teachers.
10. Assists students in locating information and resources valuable to their educational needs and to the growth of their personal interests and ability.
11. Helps students and teachers find and use relevant information sources outside the school.
12. Provides interlibrary loan services to students.
13. Provides interlibrary loan services to teachers.
14. Provides reading/listening/viewing guidance to students.
15. Helps parents realize the importance of assisting their children to understand the benefits of reading, listening, and viewing for pleasure as well as for gaining information.
16. Coordinates in-school production of materials required for instructional use and other activities.
17. Provides technical assistance to students in the production of materials.
18. Provides technical assistance to teachers in the production of materials.
19. Coordinates textbook selection, ordering, and distribution program in school.
20. Coordinates school-operated radio station.
21. Coordinates video production activities in school.
22. Coordinates cable or other TV transmission and utilization activities in school.

**TABLE A1.**    High Service Programs in Elementary Schools under 500

| | Percentile Level | | |
| --- | --- | --- | --- |
| *Staff* | *75* | *90* | *95* |
| Full-time Equivalent (FTE) Certified Professional Staff | 1.0 | 1.0 | 1.0 |
| FTE Other Professional Staff | .0 | .5 | 1.0 |
| FTE Nonprofessional Staff | 1.0 | 1.0 | 1.1 |
| FTE Total Paid Staff (Professional & Nonprofessional) | 1.5 | 2.0 | 2.0 |
| FTE Adult Volunteers | 2.0 | 10.0 | 30.0 |
| FTE Student Volunteers | 2.0 | 5.0 | 10.0 |

| *Collection* | | | |
| --- | --- | --- | --- |
| Number of Books Held, End '85 (Volumes) | 9227 | 11,117 | 12,809 |
| Total Book Titles Held per Pupil | 23 | 31 | 38 |
| Number of Serials Held, End '85 (Titles) | 28 | 43 | 50 |
| Subscriptions Held per 100 Pupils | 9 | 12 | 16 |
| Number of Microforms Held, End '85 (Titles) | 0 | 35 | 355 |
| Number of Audio Titles Held, End '85 | 546 | 904 | 1183 |
| Number of Film, Filmstrip Titles Held, End of '85 | 741 | 1159 | 1542 |
| Number of Video Tape Titles Held, End '85 | 21 | 70 | 122 |
| Machine-Readable Titles (Computer) Held, End of '85 | 52 | 100 | 198 |
| Other Materials Held, End '85 (Titles) | 330 | 970 | 1616 |

| *Facilities & Equipment* | | | |
| --- | --- | --- | --- |
| Number of Microcomputers under Supervision of the Library Media Center | 6 | 12 | 18 |
| Net Area (in square feet) for Library Media Center | 2320 | 3500 | 4406 |
| Number of Seats Available in Library Media Center | 50 | 70 | 75 |

| *Budget* | | | |
| --- | --- | --- | --- |
| Book Budget per Pupil | $ 7.74 | $11.49 | $16.73 |
| Serial Budget per Pupil | 1.31 | 1.85 | 2.67 |
| Microform Budget per Pupil | .00 | .00 | .00 |
| Software Budget per Pupil | 1.82 | 3.03 | 4.78 |
| Audiovisual Budget per Pupil | 2.92 | 5.26 | 6.82 |
| Film Rental Budget per Pupil | .00 | .80 | 1.10 |

| | | | |
| --- | --- | --- | --- |
| Total Collection Budget per Pupil | $13.98 | $19.46 | $24.42 |
| Total Hardware Budget per Pupil | 5.51 | 10.79 | 16.59 |
| Total Library Media Budget per Pupil | 23.40 | 33.22 | 40.63 |

**TABLE A2.**    High Service Programs in Elementary Schools over 500

| Staff | Percentile Level | | |
|---|---|---|---|
| | 75 | 90 | 95 |
| Full-time Equivalent (FTE) Certified Professional Staff | 1.0 | 1.0 | 1.0 |
| FTE Other Professional Staff | .0 | .2 | 1.0 |
| FTE Nonprofessional Staff | 1.0 | 1.0 | 2.0 |
| FTE Total Paid Staff (Professional & Nonprofessional) | 2.0 | 2.0 | 2.7 |
| FTE Adult Volunteers | 5.0 | 19.8 | 41.0 |
| FTE Student Volunteers | 1.0 | 5.0 | 7.8 |

| Collection | | | |
|---|---|---|---|
| Number of Books Held, End '85 (Volumes) | 11,386 | 15,009 | 17,280 |
| Total Book Titles Held per Pupil | 15 | 20 | 27 |
| Number of Serials Held, End '85 (Titles) | 32 | 49 | 67 |
| Subscriptions Held per 100 Pupils | 5 | 8 | 10 |
| Number of Microforms Held, End '85 (Titles) | 0 | 3 | 148 |
| Number of Audio Titles Held, End '85 | 773 | 1212 | 1592 |
| Number of Film, Filmstrip Titles Held, End of '85 | 1009 | 1741 | 2443 |
| Number of Video Tape Titles Held, End '85 | 30 | 62 | 100 |
| Machine-Readable Titles (Computer) Held, End of '85 | 81 | 129 | 204 |
| Other Materials Held, End '85 (Titles) | 718 | 1593 | 2434 |

| Facilities & Equipment | | | |
|---|---|---|---|
| Number of Microcomputers under Supervision of the Library Media Center | 6 | 11 | 15 |
| Net Area (in square feet) for Library Media Center | 3366 | 5145 | 6153 |
| Number of Seats Available in Library Media Center | 67 | 84 | 97 |

| Budget | | | |
|---|---|---|---|
| Book Budget per Pupil | $ 5.83 | $ 7.54 | $11.92 |
| Serial Budget per Pupil | .88 | 1.32 | 1.70 |
| Microform Budget per Pupil | .00 | .00 | .00 |
| Software Budget per Pupil | 1.08 | 2.12 | 2.69 |
| Audiovisual Budget per Pupil | 2.44 | 3.63 | 5.82 |
| Film Rental Budget per Pupil | .00 | .74 | 1.52 |

| | | | |
|---|---|---|---|
| Total Collection Budget per Pupil | $10.47 | $14.93 | $18.34 |
| Total Hardware Budget per Pupil | 3.69 | 9.27 | 15.68 |
| Total Library Media Budget per Pupil | 18.13 | 27.26 | 34.94 |

TABLE A3.    High Service Programs in Middle/Junior High Schools
with Enrollments under 500

| Staff | Percentile Level | | |
|---|---|---|---|
| | 75 | 90 | 95 |
| Full-time Equivalent (FTE) Certified Professional Staff | 1.0 | 1.0 | 1.2 |
| FTE Other Professional Staff | .0 | .1 | .8 |
| FTE Nonprofessional Staff | .8 | 1.0 | 1.0 |
| FTE Total Paid Staff (Professional & Nonprofessional) | 2.0 | 2.0 | 2.0 |
| FTE Adult Volunteers | .0 | 2.8 | 5.8 |
| FTE Student Volunteers | 7.8 | 21.0 | 33.3 |

| Collection | | | |
|---|---|---|---|
| Number of Books Held, End '85 (Volumes) | 10,015 | 12,933 | 14,178 |
| Total Book Titles Held per Pupil | 25 | 30 | 34 |
| Number of Serials Held, End '85 | 45 | 79 | 87 |
| Total Subscriptions Held per 100 Students | 12 | 21 | 24 |
| Number of Microforms Held, End '85 (Titles) | 0 | 57 | 1200 |
| Number of Audio Titles Held, End '85 | 478 | 927 | 1552 |
| Number of Film, Filmstrip Titles Held, End of '85 | 1031 | 1343 | 2050 |
| Number of Video Tape Titles Held, End '85 | 45 | 179 | 257 |
| Machine-Readable Titles (Computer) Held, End '85 | 50 | 86 | 137 |
| Other Materials Held, End '85 (Titles) | 547 | 1800 | 3584 |

| Facilities & Equipment | | | |
|---|---|---|---|
| Number of Microcomputers under Supervision of the Library Media Center | 3 | 8 | 20 |
| Net Area (in square feet) for Library Media Center | 3200 | 4202 | 4605 |
| Number of Seats Available in Library Media Center | 72 | 88 | 93 |

| Budget | | | |
|---|---|---|---|
| Book Budget per Pupil | $10.14 | $15.05 | $18.74 |
| Serial Budget per Pupil | 3.10 | 4.74 | 5.89 |
| Microform Budget per Pupil | .00 | .00 | .08 |
| Software Budget per Pupil | 1.79 | 3.10 | 4.51 |
| Audiovisual Budget per Pupil | 3.78 | 5.97 | 6.83 |
| Film Rental Budget per Pupil | .47 | 2.38 | 3.86 |

| | | | |
|---|---|---|---|
| Total Collection Budget per Pupil | $18.67 | $28.42 | $33.83 |
| Total Hardware Budget per Pupil | 3.23 | 6.96 | 18.43 |
| Total Library Media Budget per Pupil | 32.10 | 44.34 | 58.26 |

**TABLE A4.**    High Service Programs in Middle/Junior High Schools over 500

| Staff | Percentile Level | | |
|---|---|---|---|
| | 75 | 90 | 95 |
| Full-time Equivalent (FTE) Certified Professional Staff | 1.0 | 2.0 | 2.0 |
| FTE Other Professional Staff | .0 | .0 | 1.0 |
| FTE Nonprofessional Staff | 1.0 | 1.0 | 1.6 |
| FTE Total Paid Staff (Professional & Nonprofessional) | 2.0 | 3.0 | 4.0 |
| FTE Adult Volunteers | .0 | 2.9 | 8.4 |
| FTE Student Volunteers | 10.0 | 20.0 | 26.7 |

| Collection | | | |
|---|---|---|---|
| Number of Books Held, End '85 (Volumes) | 13,996 | 16,375 | 18,540 |
| Total Book Titles Held per Pupil | 16 | 19 | 23 |
| Number of Serials Held, End '85 (Titles) | 73 | 90 | 114 |
| Subscriptions Held per 100 Pupils | 9 | 12 | 17 |
| Number of Microforms Held, End '85 (Titles) | 12 | 1111 | 4438 |
| Number of Audio Titles Held, End '85 | 538 | 1210 | 1760 |
| Number of Film, Filmstrip Titles Held, End of '85 | 996 | 1627 | 2061 |
| Number of Video Tape Titles Held, End '85 | 41 | 87 | 160 |
| Machine-Readable Titles (Computer) Held, End of '85 | 68 | 119 | 159 |
| Other Materials Held, End '85 (Titles) | 753 | 2056 | 2804 |

| Facilities & Equipment | | | |
|---|---|---|---|
| Number of Microcomputers under Supervision of the Library Media Center | 4 | 13 | 26 |
| Net Area (in square feet) for Library Media Center | 5946 | 7583 | 8771 |
| Number of Seats Available in Library Media Center | 102 | 140 | 170 |

| Budget | | | |
|---|---|---|---|
| Book Budget per Pupil | $ 6.82 | $10.49 | $12.08 |
| Serial Budget per Pupil | 1.71 | 2.51 | 2.97 |
| Microform Budget per Pupil | .00 | .20 | .48 |
| Software Budget per Pupil | .99 | 1.88 | 3.15 |
| Audiovisual Budget per Pupil | 2.16 | 3.37 | 3.88 |
| Film Rental Budget per Pupil | .05 | .58 | 1.32 |

| | | | |
|---|---|---|---|
| Total Collection Budget per Pupil | $11.92 | $17.27 | $19.73 |
| Total Hardware Budget per Pupil | 1.97 | 9.06 | 19.37 |
| Total Library Media Budget per Pupil | 23.05 | 30.68 | 37.26 |

**TABLE A5.**    High Service Programs in High Schools with Enrollments under 500

| Staff | Percentile Level | | |
|---|---|---|---|
| | 75 | 90 | 95 |
| Full-time Equivalent (FTE) Certified Professional Staff | 1.0 | 1.0 | 1.0 |
| FTE Other Professional Staff | .0 | .0 | .2 |
| FTE Nonprofessional Staff | .8 | 1.0 | 2.6 |
| FTE Total Paid Staff (Professional & Nonprofessional) | 1.8 | 2.0 | 3.6 |
| FTE Adult Volunteers | .0 | .0 | 9.6 |
| FTE Student Volunteers | 15.5 | 20.0 | 48.5 |

| Collection | | | |
|---|---|---|---|
| Number of Books Held, End '85 (Volumes) | 10,422 | 13,065 | 14,808 |
| Total Book Titles Held per Pupil | 34 | 51 | 58 |
| Number of Serials Held, End '85 | 72 | 108 | 112 |
| Total Subscriptions Held per 100 Students | 25 | 34 | 55 |
| Number of Microforms Held, End '85 | 137 | 850 | 1735 |
| Number of Audio Titles Held, End '85 | 591 | 1385 | 2232 |
| Number of Film, Filmstrip Titles Held, End of '85 | 603 | 1190 | 1792 |
| Number of Video Tape Titles Held, End '85 | 57 | 186 | 310 |
| Machine-Readable Titles (Computer) Held, End '85 | 60 | 128 | 238 |
| Other Materials Held, End '85 (Titles) | 491 | 2100 | 2353 |

| Facilities & Equipment | | | |
|---|---|---|---|
| Number of Microcomputers under Supervision of the Library Media Center | 2 | 11 | 13 |
| Net Area (in square feet) for Library Media Center | 3626 | 5280 | 8875 |
| Number of Seats Available in Library Media Center | 79 | 97 | 100 |

| Budget | | | |
|---|---|---|---|
| Book Budget per Pupil | $12.17 | $25.23 | $31.54 |
| Serial Budget per Pupil | 4.72 | 8.23 | 11.36 |
| Microform Budget per Pupil | .00 | .71 | 1.43 |
| Software Budget per Pupil | 1.55 | 5.35 | 9.68 |
| Audiovisual Budget per Pupil | 5.32 | 7.32 | 13.65 |
| Film Rental Budget per Pupil | .61 | 2.89 | 3.30 |

| | | | |
|---|---|---|---|
| Total Collection Budget per Pupil | $27.62 | $44.58 | $59.65 |
| Total Hardware Budget per Pupil | 2.77 | 9.16 | 23.84 |
| Total Library Media Budget per Pupil | 42.49 | 72.21 | 92.68 |

**TABLE A6.**    High Service Programs in High Schools with Enrollments between 500 and 1000

| Staff | Percentile Level | | |
|---|---|---|---|
| | 75 | 90 | 95 |
| Full-time Equivalent (FTE) Certified Professional Staff | 1.0 | 2.0 | 2.0 |
| FTE Other Professional Staff | .0 | .6 | 1.0 |
| FTE Nonprofessional Staff | 1.0 | 2.5 | 3.1 |
| FTE Total Paid Staff (Professional & Nonprofessional) | 3.0 | 4.0 | 5.1 |
| FTE Adult Volunteers | .0 | .2 | 8.3 |
| FTE Student Volunteers | 18.8 | 26.0 | 28.5 |

| Collection | | | |
|---|---|---|---|
| Number of Books Held, End '85 (Volumes) | 16,320 | 22,821 | 25,939 |
| Total Book Titles Held per Pupil | 19 | 25 | 29 |
| Number of Serials Held, End '85 (Titles) | 116 | 150 | 197 |
| Subscriptions Held per 100 Pupils | 15 | 25 | 26 |
| Number of Microforms Held, End '85 (Titles) | 455 | 2144 | 4547 |
| Number of Audio Titles Held, End '85 | 597 | 1104 | 1993 |
| Number of Film, Filmstrip Titles Held, End of '85 | 1025 | 1448 | 1686 |
| Number of Video Tape Titles Held, End '85 | 72 | 129 | 253 |
| Machine-Readable Titles (Computer) Held, End of '85 | 19 | 89 | 286 |
| Other Materials Held, End '85 (Titles) | 299 | 2122 | 3701 |

| Facilities & Equipment | | | |
|---|---|---|---|
| Number of Microcomputers under Supervision of the Library Media Center | 1 | 6 | 8 |
| Net Area (in square feet) for Library Media Center | 5591 | 9625 | 10,139 |
| Number of Seats Available in Library Media Center | 120 | 164 | 206 |

| Budget | | | |
|---|---|---|---|
| Book Budget per Pupil | $ 8.80 | $12.97 | $17.69 |
| Serial Budget per Pupil | 3.49 | 5.36 | 7.47 |
| Microform Budget per Pupil | .06 | .76 | .81 |
| Software Budget per Pupil | .46 | 1.13 | 1.84 |
| Audiovisual Budget per Pupil | 2.72 | 4.29 | 7.50 |
| Film Rental Budget per Pupil | .89 | 2.41 | 4.36 |

| | | | |
|---|---|---|---|
| Total Collection Budget per Pupil | $18.42 | $23.71 | $25.76 |
| Total Hardware Budget per Pupil | 2.08 | 4.09 | 7.08 |
| Total Library Media Budget per Pupil | 21.77 | 34.16 | 44.52 |

**TABLE A7.**    High Service Programs in High Schools with Enrollments
over 1000

| Staff | Percentile Level | | |
|---|---|---|---|
| | 75 | 90 | 95 |
| Full-time Equivalent (FTE) Certified Professional Staff | 2.0 | 3.0 | 3.0 |
| FTE Other Professional Staff | .0 | .1 | 1.0 |
| FTE Nonprofessional Staff | 2.8 | 3.8 | 5.1 |
| FTE Total Paid Staff (Professional & Nonprofessional) | 4.7 | 6.0 | 8.0 |
| FTE Adult Volunteers | .0 | 2.4 | 5.0 |
| FTE Student Volunteers | 18.8 | 34.4 | 47.4 |

| Collection | | | |
|---|---|---|---|
| Number of Books Held, End '85 (Volumes) | 23,745 | 30,500 | 37,668 |
| Total Book Titles Held per Pupil | 14 | 17 | 21 |
| Number of Serials Held, End '85 | 145 | 198 | 231 |
| Total Subscriptions Held per 100 Students | 10 | 14 | 15 |
| Number of Microforms Held, End '85 | 2125 | 8011 | 24,384 |
| Number of Audio Titles Held, End '85 | 1005 | 1653 | 2410 |
| Number of Film, Filmstrip Titles Held, End of '85 | 1391 | 2500 | 2877 |
| Number of Video Tape Titles Held, End '85 | 172 | 356 | 519 |
| Machine-Readable Titles (Computer) Held, End '85 | 37 | 154 | 236 |
| Other Materials Held, End '85 (Titles) | 957 | 2260 | 10,499 |

| Facilities & Equipment | | | |
|---|---|---|---|
| Number of Microcomputers under Supervision of the Library Media Center | 3 | 8 | 11 |
| Net Area (in square feet) for Library Media Center | 9462 | 12,954 | 14,984 |
| Number of Seats Available in Library Media Center | 172 | 211 | 253 |

| Budget | | | |
|---|---|---|---|
| Book Budget per Pupil | $ 7.31 | $11.59 | $13.73 |
| Serial Budget per Pupil | 2.11 | 2.94 | 4.95 |
| Microform Budget per Pupil | .18 | .67 | 1.09 |
| Software Budget per Pupil | .42 | 1.49 | 3.45 |
| Audiovisual Budget per Pupil | 2.51 | 3.94 | 5.36 |
| Film Rental Budget per Pupil | .57 | 2.06 | 3.23 |

| | | | |
|---|---|---|---|
| Total Collection Budget per Pupil | $14.63 | $19.71 | $24.16 |
| Total Hardware Budget per Pupil | 1.08 | 4.14 | 8.58 |
| Total Library Media Budget per Pupil | 18.34 | 27.45 | 39.31 |

# Budget Formulas for Materials and Equipment

## Formula for Calculating Materials Budget*

### *Formula:*

$$MB = C \times (1 \pm V + Aw + Ad + Al) \times (1 + I)$$

This formula represents one way to calculate budgetary needs for maintenance of the current building-level media center materials allocation. The formula is not intended to take into account special needs for enhancing the budget, such as those occasioned by extensive curriculum revisions, textbook changes, lower than appropriate materials expenditures, and so on. Additional expenditure amounts should be allocated for specific nonperiodic needs.

Dollar amounts used in the formula should be based on the building allocation of funds for all forms of media, excluding equipment. Materials covered by this formula are library media center books and audiovisual materials, including microcomputer software, periodicals, reference materials, and microfilm.

### *Category Definitions*

$MB$ = Materials budget for the upcoming year
$C$   = Amount spent for media in the current year
$V$   = Variation in student population
$Aw$ = Attrition by weeding
$Ad$ = Attrition by date
$Al$  = Attrition by loss
$I$    = Inflation rate

*Quoted with permission from: Dianne M. Hopkins, Leslyn Shires, M. Elaine Anderson, and Richard J. Sorenson. *School Library Media Programs: A Resource and Planning Guide*, pp. 65–66. Wisconsin Department of Public Instruction, 1987.

### *Criteria*

V—Variation in Student Population. This is the change in the number of students served. Calculate this number using the equation below. It will be added if it represents an increase or subtracted if it represents a decrease.

(increase or decrease) V original × 0.2 =

Aw—Attrition by Weeding. The attrition by weeding is determined using the percent of the collection that has been weeded.

| % of Collection Weeded | Add to Formula |
|---|---|
| 0 to 1.99% | 0.00 |
| 2 to 4.99% | 0.01 |
| 5 to 9.99% | 0.02 |
| 10% or more | 0.03 |

Ad—Attrition by Date. This will indicate the age of the collection. Do a systematic sampling of the collection of print and audiovisual nonfiction materials. One sampling procedure is described below.

Assume that 100 cards in the shelflist equal one inch. Select a sample of approximately 200 items using these steps.

1. Estimate the size of the nonfiction collection. First, measure the shelflist with a ruler and estimate that each inch represents 100 cards. For example, a nonfiction shelflist that measures about 40 inches suggests that the nonfiction collection includes about 4,000 items.

2. Divide the size of the nonfiction collection (in inches) by the size of the sample desired. This produces the sampling interval. Convert the resulting number to sixteenths of an inch to make measuring the shelflist easier. A 200-item sample is probably large enough to ensure that judgments based upon it will be accurate. For example, to sample 200 titles from a 40-inch nonfiction collection, divide 40 by 200. The sampling interval is 0.2, or $^3/_{16}$ of an inch.

3. Using the calculated sampling interval, pull shelflist cards and note the latest copyright date of each title selected. Determine the percentage of the nonfiction collection that is 15 years old or older and then add the appropriate number to the formula.

| % of Nonfiction Collection 15+ Years | Add to Formula |
|---|---|
| 0 to  2.99% | 0.00 |
| 3 to  4.99% | 0.01 |
| 5 to  9.99% | 0.02 |
| 10 to 19.99% | 0.03 |
| 20% or more | 0.04 |

A1—Attrition by Loss. Every year, a number of items cannot be accounted for and may be declared lost. Add a number to the formula based upon the percentage of the collection that has been lost.

| % of Collection Lost | Add to Formula |
|---|---|
| 0 to .99% | 0.00 |
| 1 to 1.99% | 0.01 |
| 2 to 2.99% | 0.02 |
| 3% or more | 0.03 |

I—Inflation. The latest inflation rate percent of change listed in the Consumer Price Index can be used in the formula. Another source is the most current edition of a world almanac.

An alternative is to identify the inflation rate for books and other media and to use those figures or an average of them. The choice is up to those using the formula. It is important to be consistent once the choice of inflation rate has been made.

For the sake of illustration, imagine a building media center collection that includes 15,000 media items of all types. Last year, the center's total materials budget was $4,800; it served 400 students.

The school enrollment increased by 23 students; 289 books were lost and 241 weeded. Sixty of 400 randomly selected items were found to be 15 years old or older. The inflation rate for the last year was 0.038.

Those using the formula above to calculate the materials budget for the coming year must first determine the numbers that will go into the formula.

C   = $4,800
V   = Increase of 23 students
      23 V 400 = 0.0575 increase in student population
      $0.0575 \times 0.2 = 0.0115$, so add 0.0115
Aw = 242 items weeded from a collection of 15,000 items
      242 V 15,000 = 0.016
      This is less than 2 percent, so add nothing.
Ad = For a collection of 12,000 nonfiction books (15,000 items minus 3000 fiction titles), 320 cards were checked and 60 found to be for items 15 years old or older.
      60 V 320 = 0.1875
      18.75 percent is over 10 percent, so add 0.03.
A1 = 289 books were unaccounted for out of the 15,000-item collection
      289 V 15,000 = 0.019
      1.9 percent is between 1 percent and 2 percent of the collection, so add 0.01.
I    = The inflation rate listed was 0.038.

Now the variables can be used in the formula.

$$MB = C \times (1 \pm V + Aw + Ad + A1) \times (1 + I)$$
$$= \$4,800 \times (1 + 0.0115 + 0.00 + 0.03 + 0.01) \times (1 + 0.038)$$
$$= (\$4,800 \times 1.0515) \times (1.038)$$
$$= \$5,047.20 \times 1.038$$
$$MB = \$5,238.99$$

For justification purposes, the new materials budget should be $5,238.99.

## Formula for Calculating Equipment Budget*

### Formula:

$$EB = C \times AA + R(V)(I)$$

### Category Definitions

EB = Equipment budget
C = Current inventory replacement value
AA = Average age of equipment
R = Replacement value for lost, stolen, or damaged items
I = Inflation rate

Example: Value of the current inventory is $100,000 and the average age is seven years. One VCR was damaged beyond repair during the year; replacement cost is $315. Rate of inflation is figured at 1.2 percent.

$$\$100,000 \times 7 = \$700,000 \times .012 = \$8400 + \$315 = \$8715 \ EB$$

For a new school with the same inventory, the budget would be:

$$\$100,000 \times .012 = \$1200 \ EB.$$

## Alternative Method for Calculating Budgets for Library Books and Periodicals**

Traditionally, expenditures for library books and periodicals have been recommended only in terms of dollars per pupil. As a very general guide this may be effective; however, there are several factors that will affect the appropriateness of such a guideline.

Most important is the current status of the library media program. Before a program budget can be deemed appropriate, it must be examined with respect to its ability to respond to the curriculum needs of the school and to what is considered good practice for school library media

*This formula was constructed following the ideas formulated in the materials budget formula.

**Used with permission of the Connecticut State Education Department, Hartford.

programs. What may be an adequate expenditure for a school with a library media collection that is current and sufficient in breadth and depth may be woefully lacking in a school that is trying to improve its collection or in a program that has been neglected.

Another factor is the decrease that each school collection will sustain each year due to loss, damage, or wear that is beyond repair. Approximately 5 percent of a collection must be replaced annually for these reasons. Costs for replacement of old materials and addition of new materials will be affected by current prices, a factor that determines what the dollars will actually buy. For example, over the past few years book prices have increased at a rate greater than the general inflation rate for the nation.

Additionally, the school population affects the adequacy of per pupil recommendation. A minimum collection must be maintained regardless of the number of students in the school. Consequently, an extremely small school may find that additional funds per pupil may be necessary.

Given those factors, the following model is presented as a guide for calculating budget recommendations for the print section of the library media budget.

Factor A:  Replacement of books lost, damaged, out of date, or containing inaccurate information

5% × Number of books in the collection × Average price of a library book for the school level                    $_____

Factor B:  Periodical Subscriptions

Number of periodical subscriptions × Average price of a periodical subscription for the school level or
Actual cost for subscriptions needed          $_____

Factor C:  Growth and expansion of the book collection based on the current status of the collection

1. If the book collection fulfills 90% or more of state guidelines, use 3%–5%
2. If the book collection fulfills between 75% and 90% of guidelines, use 10%–15%
3. If the book collection falls below 75% of state guidelines, use 15%–25%

Percentage × Number of books in the collection × Average price of a library book for the school level          $_____

Factor D:   Reference materials

Actual dollar amount for the materials
needed                                                   $_____

As an example, this formula can be applied to a model elementary school of 250 pupils and 20 staff. It is assumed that the library media center contains a basic collection of resources that meet curriculum and leisure needs of students and staff. There are 6,000 volumes in the book collection.

Factor A:   5% or 300 volumes would need to be replaced due to loss, damage, or wear that
cannot be repaired. The average price of an
elementary-level hardbound book is $12.00
for both fiction and nonfiction.
.05 × 6,000 = 300
300 × $12.00 = $3,600                                    $3,600

Factor B:   25 periodical subscriptions need to be renewed or started. The average price of an
elementary-level periodical subscription is
$11.00.
25 × $11.00 = $275.00                                    $  275

Factor C:   3% or 180 volumes would be added to the
collection to supply new leisure reading and
to give greater breadth and depth to the
collection. The average price of an elementary library book is $12.00.
.03 × 6,000 = 180
180 × $12.00 = 2,160                                     $2,160

Factor D:   A new addition of an encyclopedia and
other reference books totals $750.00                    $  750

Total amount requested
for library books and
periodicals                                             $6,785

This formula may also be applied to middle school, junior high, and high school budgets, using the average costs for books and periodicals for the appropriate academic level. Prices vary by level and tend to increase each year.

In addition to mere numbers that would indicate the need for increased budgeting, there are other variables that will affect the budget request for library books and periodicals.

1. *Age of the collection.* Though adequate in number of volumes, careful examination may reveal many books that need to be removed from the collection because there are newer additions or unnecessary duplications or because the content is no longer accurate or complete.

2. *Strengths and weaknesses.* Though adequate in size, the collection may not meet the needs of all curriculum areas. Special budget increases may be needed when a curriculum area is revised or new courses are introduced.
3. *Changes in the school population.* Situations that lead to a substantial increase in the number, type, or grade level of the student population may require a special infusion of funds to supply resources that meet their learning needs.
4. *Inflation.* Library books and periodicals have increased at a rate greater than the national inflation rate, and so each dollar buys less as time goes by.

These variables should be considered when developing a recommendation for the library books and periodicals portion of the budget. The resulting amount should then be included with other areas of the library media program such as audiovisual materials, computer programs, new technology, audiovisual equipment, and supplies to give a total budget request.

# Library Media Facilities Guidelines

The physical space allocated to library media programs is an important element in the provision of an effective school library media program. Adequate, attractive space encourages the use of the center.

The space recommendations below have allowed for flexibility to reflect differences in educational programs and in the size of the school. Each library media center should be planned in conjunction with the total educational requirements of the school.

TABLE C1.    Library Media Center Space Recommendations

| Area/ Function | Relationships/ Considerations | Space Allocation in Square Feet | |
|---|---|---|---|
| | | 500 Students | 1000 Students |
| Entrance/Circulation | Near entrance—reserve section, workroom. Card catalog/on-line terminals, periodical/nonprint storage, equipment storage. | 250–500 | 600–800 |
| | Should have facilities for displays, copy machine, charge area. Program may warrant additional satellite areas for some services such as copy machine, microform readers, etc. | | |
| Reading, browsing, listening, viewing, individual study, computing | Near card catalog/on-line terminals, reference area, magazines microform readers and periodical indexes. In elementary schools, the storytelling area should be located away from circulation area. | 25–75% according to program requirements | 25–75% Same |
| | Adequate shelving should be provided for 10 items per ft. At least 25% of the area should be available for student seating allowing 40 sq. ft. per student. | | |

The instructional programs in some schools may require that 1/3 to 3/4 of the student population be accommodated in the library media center. No more than 100 students should be seated in one area.

Mixed seating should include tables and chairs, carrels and lounge-type seating. Some seating should be provided in carrels or equipped tables. Carrels require approximately 16 sq. ft. floor space each to accommodate a computer and printer.

Provision should be made for electrical outlets, telephone and tv reception. Electrical outlets should be switch-controlled at charge desk.

Consideration should be given to a flexible system for electrical cable, coaxial cable, and such as a cable duct under the floor or a floor. Computer terminals for data base should be provided.

In addition to the facilities for individual listening and viewing in the carrels in the mail library media areas, small group listening and viewing areas are often necessary. The areas should have electrical outlets, provision for television outlets, light control, wall screen (few if any windows), acoustical treatment.

Small group areas—listening and viewing

150
1–3 areas

Same

| Area/Function | Relationships/Considerations | Space Allocation in Square Feet | |
|---|---|---|---|
| | | 500 Students | 1000 Students |
| Equipment storage and distribution | Near corridor, loading dock and elevator. | 400–600 | 500–800 |
| | Should have good control from work area. | | |
| | Near production, carrel and viewing areas. | | |
| | Should be in a secure area. | | |
| | Cabinets with locks need to be provided for storage of equipment and supplies. | | |
| | Should have electrical outlets. | | |
| | Should have shelving and tables. | | |
| Maintenance repair | Near loading dock, elevators, corridor, adjacent to equipment, storage and distribution | 150–300 | Same |
| | Secure area. | | |
| | Include workbench, electrical, and television outlets. | | |
| | Storage for parts, lamps, equipment under repair. | | |
| | Provision for necessary test equipment. | | |
| | Consider locating adjacent to equipment storage. | | |
| Media production laboratory | Secure area. | 50–700 | 700–900 |
| | Provide housing for equipment and materials used in production, and shelving and storage for supplies. | | |

| | | | |
|---|---|---|---|
| Darkroom | Requires refrigeration, sinks, running water, electrical outlets, and counter space. | 150–300 | Same |
| | Sound control is needed for audio production. | | |
| | Plan space arrangements in terms of production methods used and work flow. | | |
| | The darkroom area should be adjacent to the media production laboratory. (A darkroom may be provided elsewhere in the school.) | | |
| | Requires sinks, running water, electrical outlets, light locks, refrigeration, counter space, adequate ventilation. | | |
| Conference areas | Locate in quiet and easily supervised area. | 150<br>2–4 areas | Same |
| | An online search station should be placed near the conference rooms. | | |
| | Should be acoustically treated and equipped with electrical and television outlets and a permanent screen. | | |
| | At least one room should be equipped with a computer and one with a typewriter. | | |
| | Should have moveable walls to allow for combining areas. | | |
| | May be used to house special collections which are used frequently. | | |
| | Should be equipped with multipurpose use—see listening and viewing. | | |
| | The listening and viewing areas and the conference areas can serve multiple functions. | | |

| Area/Function | Relationships/Considerations | Space Allocation in Square Feet | |
|---|---|---|---|
| | | 500 Students | 1000 Students |
| Multipurpose room | Adjacent to reference area, stack area, catalogs, and indexes. | 700–900 | 900–1200 |
| | Good visual control from main library media area and workroom is essential. | | |
| | Space should be flexible and at least classroom size, and equipped for presentation using all forms of media. | | |
| | Telephone jack for telephone conference and computer terminal. | | |
| | Computer should be available. | | |
| Work area | Near entrance, circulation, periodical/nonprint storage. | 200–400 | 300–500 |
| | Near instructional/group project area. | | |
| | Should have access to corridor. | | |
| | Desk space for library media professionals should be provided here or in an appropriate area of the library media center. | | |
| | Provision for shelving, counters, cabinets, sink, running, water, electrical outlets, telephone, copy equipment and computer access. | | |
| | Additional space may be required if cataloging is to be done in the school. | | |

| | | | |
|---|---|---|---|
| Periodical storage | Near entrance, circulation, microform readers and reader printers. | 250–400 | 400–600 |
| | Copy equipment should be in close proximity. | | |
| | Magazine indexes, such as *Magazine Index* or *Texts of Microfilm*, should be close to the magazine storage area. | | |
| | Periodicals on microfilm should be provided to allow access to a larger collection in less space. | | |
| | Cabinets should be provided to house microform. Compact shelving should be considered to save space. | | |
| Teacher/professional area | Near classrooms, teachers' office, main library media area, quiet area. | 500–600 | 600–800 |
| | Plan for use as faculty group meeting or conference area. | | |
| | Provide for listening and viewing and for selection and evaluation of new materials and equipment. | | |
| | Emphasize lounge atmosphere. | | |
| | Equip with telephone, computer, typewriter, listening and viewing equipment, professional journals and other resources. | | |
| Computer learning laboratory | Adjacent to group project and instruction area. | 600–800 | 800–1000 |
| | Secure area. | | |
| | Should have response capability. | | |
| | Size of space may vary with nature of computer program. | | |

| Area/Function | Relationships/Considerations | Space Allocation in Square Feet | |
|---|---|---|---|
| | | 500 Students | 1000 Students |
| Stacks | Locate near reserve area, if appropriate. | 400 minimum | 400–600 |
| | Consider location in relation to periodical storage. | | |
| | Adequate lighting. | | |
| | Provide for tables and seating as necessary, depending on types of materials sorted in stacks. | | |
| | Include additional stack space as needed to store textbooks. | | |
| Television studio | Should be convenient to media production. | 1,600 studio 40′ × 40′ with 15′ ceiling, wide doors | Same |
| | Area must be soundproof. | | |
| | Classroom facilities may be needed. | | |
| | Studio capability may be provided instead at district level. | | |
| | Consider as alternatives for school television production: mini-studios and portable video-tape units. | | |
| | Secure area. | | |
| Audio studio | Should be located adjacent to television studio. | 150 minimum | Same |
| | Area must be soundproof. | | |
| | Provision for storage of equipment and supplies. | | |
| | Secure area. | | |

| | | |
|---|---|---|
| Telecommunications distribution | Adjacent to television studio and equipment repair.<br><br>Provision for equipment neccesary to distribute audio and visual programs—editing equipment room, TV and audio.<br><br>Secure area. | 800 minimum | Same |

# Policies and Statements on Access to Information

## Library Bill of Rights

The American Library Association affirms that all libraries are forums for information and ideas, and that the following basic policies should guide their services.

1. Books and other library resources should be provided for the interest, information, and enlightenment of all people of the community the library serves. Materials should not be excluded because of the origin, background, or views of those contributing to their creation.

2. Libraries should provide materials and information presenting all points of view on current and historical issues. Materials should not be proscribed or removed because of partisan and doctrinal disapproval.

3. Libraries should challenge censorship in the fulfillment of their responsibility to provide information and enlightenment.

4. Libraries should cooperate with all persons and groups concerned with resisting abridgment of free expression and free access to ideas.

5. A person's right to use a library should not be denied or abridged because of origin, age, background, or views.

6. Libraries which make exhibit spaces and meeting rooms available to the public they serve should make such facilities available on an equitable basis, regardless of the beliefs or affiliations of individuals or groups requesting their use.

Adopted June 18, 1948. Amended February 2, 1981, June 27, 1967 and January 23, 1980, by the ALA Council.

## Access to Resources and Services in the School Library Media Program
## An Interpretation of the *Library Bill of Rights*

The school library media program plays a unique role in promoting intellectual freedom. It serves as a point of voluntary access to information and ideas and as a learning laboratory for students as they acquire critical thinking and problem solving skills needed in a pluralistic society. Although the educational level and program of the school necessarily shape the resources and services of a school library media program, the principles of the LIBRARY BILL OF RIGHTS apply equally to all libraries, including school library media programs.

School library media professionals assume a leadership role in promoting the principles of intellectual freedom within the school by providing resources and services that create and sustain an atmosphere of free inquiry. School library media professionals work closely with teachers to integrate instructional activities in classroom units designed to equip students to locate, evaluate, and use a broad range of ideas effectively. Through resources, programming, and educational processes, students and teachers experience the free and robust debate characteristic of a democratic society.

School library media professionals cooperate with other individuals in building collections of resources appropriate to the developmental and maturity levels of students. These collections provide resources which support the curriculum and are consistent with the philosophy, goals, and objectives of the school district. Resources in school library media collections represent diverse points of view and current as well as historic issues.

Members of the school community involved in the collection development process employ educational criteria to select resources unfettered by their personal, political, social, or religious views. Students and educators served by the school library media program have access to resources and services free of constraints resulting from personal, partisan, doctrinal disapproval. School library media professionals resist efforts by individuals to define what is appropriate for all students or teachers to read, view, or hear.

Major barriers between students and resources include: imposing age or grade level restrictions on the use of resources, limiting the use of interlibrary loan and access to electronic information, charging fees for information in specific formats, requiring permissions from parents or teachers, establishing restricted shelves or closed collections, and

Adopted July 2, 1986, by the ALA Council

labeling. Policies, procedures and rules related to the use of resources and services support free and open access to information.

The school board adopts policies that guarantee student access to a broad range of ideas. These include policies on collection development and procedures for the review of resources about which concerns have been raised. Such policies, developed by persons in the school community, provide for a timely and fair hearing and assure that procedures are applied equitably to all expressions of concern. School library media professionals implement district policies and procedures in the school.

## AASL Statement on Confidentiality of Library Records

The members of the American Library Association,* recognizing the right to privacy of library users, believe that records held in libraries which connect specific individuals with specific resources, programs, or services, are confidential and not to be used for purposes other than routine record keeping: i.e. to maintain access to resources, to assure that resources are available to users who need them, to arrange facilities, to provide resources for the comfort and safety of patrons, or to accomplish the purposes of the program or service. The library community recognizes that children and youth have the same rights to privacy as adults.

Libraries whose record keeping systems reveal the names of users would be in violation of the confidentiality of library record laws adopted in many states. School library media specialists are advised to seek the advice of counsel if in doubt about whether their record keeping systems violate the specific laws in their states. Efforts must be made within the reasonable constraints of budgets and school management procedures to eliminate such records as soon as reasonably possible.

With or without specific legislation, school library media specialists are urged to respect the rights of children and youth by adhering to the tenets expressed in the Confidentiality of Library Records Interpretation of the Library Bill of Rights and the ALA Code of Ethics.

*ALA Policy 52.5, 54.15

## The Freedom to Read

The freedom to read is essential to our democracy. It is continuously under attack. Private groups and public authorities in various parts of the country are working to remove books from sale, to censor textbooks, to label "controversial" books, to distribute lists of "objectionable" books or authors, and to purge libraries. These actions apparently rise from a view that our national tradition of free expression is no longer valid; that censorship and suppression are needed to avoid the subversion of politics and the corruption of morals. We, as citizens devoted to the use of books and as librarians and publishers responsible for disseminating them, wish to assert the public interest in the preservation of the freedom to read.

We are deeply concerned about these attempts at suppression. Most such attempts rest on a denial of the fundamental premise of democracy: that the ordinary citizen, by exercising his critical judgment, will accept the good and reject the bad. The censors, public and private, assume that they should determine what is good and what is bad for their fellow-citizens.

We trust Americans to recognize propaganda, and to reject it. We do not believe they need the help of censors to assist them in this task. We do not believe they are prepared to sacrifice their heritage of a free press in order to be "protected" against what others think may be bad for them. We believe they still favor free enterprise in ideas and expression.

We are aware, of course, that books are not alone in being subjected to efforts at suppression. We are aware that these efforts are related to a larger pattern of pressures being brought against education, the press, films, radio, and television. The problem is not only one of actual censorship. The shadow of fear cast by these pressures leads, we suspect, to an even larger voluntary curtailment of expression by those who seek to avoid controversy.

Such pressure toward conformity is perhaps natural to a time of uneasy change and pervading fear. Especially when so many of our apprehensions are directed against an ideology, the expression of a dissident idea becomes a thing feared in itself, and we tend to move against it as against a hostile deed, with suppression.

And yet suppression is never more dangerous than in such a time

---

This statement was originally issued in May 1953 by the Westchester Conference of the American Library Association and the American Book Publishers Council, which in 1970 consolidated with the American Educational Publishers Institute to become the Association of American Publishers. Adopted June 25, 1953. Revised January 28, 1972, by the ALA Council.

of social tension. Freedom has given the United States the elasticity to endure strain. Freedom keeps open the path of novel and creative solutions, and enables change to come by choice. Every silencing of a heresy, every enforcement of an orthodoxy, diminishes the toughness and resilience of our society and leaves it the less able to deal with stress.

Now as always in our history, books are among our greatest instruments of freedom. They are almost the only means for making generally available ideas or manners of expression that can initially command only a small audience. They are the natural medium for the new idea and the untried voice from which come the original contributions to social growth. They are essential to the extended discussion which serious thought requires, and to the accumulation of knowledge and ideas into organized collections.

We believe that free communication is essential to the preservation of a free society and a creative culture. We believe that these pressures towards conformity present the danger of limiting the range and variety of inquiry and expression on which our democracy and our culture depend. We believe that every American community must jealously guard the freedom to publish and to circulate, in order to preserve its own freedom to read. We believe that publishers and librarians have a profound responsibility to give validity to that freedom to read by making it possible for the readers to choose freely from a variety of offerings.

The freedom to read is guaranteed by the Constitution. Those with faith in free men will stand firm on these constitutional guarantees of essential rights and will exercise the responsibilities that accompany these rights.

*We therefore affirm these propositions:*

1. It is in the public interest for publishers and librarians to make available the widest diversity of views and expressions, including those which are unorthodox or unpopular with the majority.

   Creative thought is by definition new, and what is new is different. The bearer of every new thought is a rebel until his idea is refined and tested. Totalitarian systems attempt to maintain themselves in power by the ruthless suppression of any concept which challenges the established orthodoxy. The power of a democratic system to adapt to change is vastly strengthened by the freedom of its citizens to choose widely from among conflicting opinions offered freely to them. To stifle every nonconformist idea at birth would mark the end of the democratic process. Furthermore, only through the constant activity of weighing and selecting can the democratic mind attain the strength demanded by times like these. We need to know not only what we believe but why we believe it.

2. Publishers, librarians, and booksellers do not need to endorse every idea or presentation contained in the books they make available. It would conflict with the public interest for them to establish their own political, moral, or aesthetic views as a standard for determining what books should be published or circulated.

   Publishers and librarians serve the educational process by helping to make available knowledge and ideas required for the growth of the mind and the increase of learning. They do not foster education by imposing as mentors the patterns of their own thought. The people should have the freedom to read and consider a broader range of ideas than those that may be held by any single librarian or publisher or government or church. It is wrong that what one man can read should be confined to what another thinks proper.

3. It is contrary to the public interest for publishers or librarians to determine the acceptability of a book on the basis of the personal history or political affiliations of the author.

   A book should be judged as a book. No art or literature can flourish if it is to be measured by the political views or private lives of its creators. No society of free men can flourish which draws up lists of writers to whom it will not listen, whatever they may have to say.

4. There is no place in our society for efforts to coerce the taste of others, to confine adults to the reading matter deemed suitable for adolescents, or to inhibit the efforts of writers to achieve artistic expression.

   To some, much of modern literature is shocking. But is not much of life itself shocking? We cut off literature at the source if we prevent writers from dealing with the stuff of life. Parents and teachers have a responsibility to prepare the young to meet the diversity of experiences in life to which they will be exposed, as they have a responsibility to help them learn to think critically for themselves. These are affirmative responsibilities, not to be discharged simply by preventing them from reading works from which they are not yet prepared. In these matters taste differs, and taste cannot be legislated; nor can machinery be devised which will suit the demands of one group without limiting the freedom of others.

5. It is not in the public interest to force a reader to accept with

any book the prejudgment of a label characterizing the book or author as subversive or dangerous.

The idea of labeling presupposes the existence of individuals or groups with wisdom to determine by authority what is good or bad for the citizen. It presupposes that each individual must be directed in making up his mind about the ideas he examines. But Americans do not need others to do their thinking for them.

6.  It is the responsibility of publishers and librarians, as guardians of the people's freedom to read, to contest encroachments upon that freedom by individuals or groups seeking to impose their own standards or tastes upon the community at large.

It is inevitable in the give and take of the democratic process that the political, the moral, or the aesthetic concepts of an individual or group will occasionally collide with those of another individual or group. In a free society each individual is free to determine for himself what he wishes to read, and each group is free to determine what it will recommend to its freely associated members. But no group has the right to take the law into its own hands, and to impose its own concept of politics or morality upon other members of a democratic society. Freedom is no freedom if it is accorded only to the accepted and the inoffensive.

7.  It is the responsibility of publishers and librarians to give full meaning to the freedom to read by providing books that enrich the quality and diversity of thought and expression. By the exercise of this affirmative responsibility, bookmen can demonstrate that the answer to a bad book is a good one, the answer to a bad idea is a good one.

The freedom to read is of little consequence when expended on the trivial; it is frustrated when the reader cannot obtain matter fit for his purpose. What is needed is not only the absence of restraint, but the positive provision of opportunity for the people to read the best that has been thought and said. Books are the major channel by which the intellectual inheritance is handed down, and the principal means of its testing and growth. The defense of their freedom and integrity, and the enlargement of their service to society, requires of all bookmen the utmost of their faculties, and deserves of all citizens the fullest of their support.

We state these propositions neither lightly nor as easy generalizations. We here stake out a lofty claim for the value of books. We do so because we believe that they are good, possessed of enormous variety and usefulness, worthy of cherishing and keeping free. We realize that the application of these propositions may mean the dissemination of ideas and manners of expression that are repugnant to many persons. We do not state these propositions in the comfortable belief that what people read is unimportant. We believe rather that what people read is deeply important; that ideas can be dangerous; but that the suppression of ideas is fatal to a democratic society. Freedom itself is a dangerous way of life, but it is ours.

## Statement on Intellectual Freedom
## The Association for Educational Communications and Technology

The First Amendment to the Constitution of the United States is a cornerstone of our liberty, supporting our rights and responsibilities regarding free speech both written and oral.

The Association for Educational Communications and Technology believes this same protection applies also to the use of sound and image in our society.

Therefore, we affirm that:

Freedom of inquiry and access to information—regardless of the format or viewpoints of the presentation—are fundamental to the development of our society. These rights must not be denied or abridged because of age, sex, race, religion, national origin, or social or political views.

Children have the right to freedom of inquiry and access to information; responsibility for abridgement of that right is solely between an individual child and the parent(s) of that child.

The need for information and the interests, growth, and enlightenment of the user should govern the selection and development of educational media, not the age, sex, race, nationality, politics, or religious doctrine of the author, producer, or publisher.

Attempts to restrict or deprive a learner's access to information representing a variety of viewpoints must be resisted as a threat to learning in a free and democratic society. Recognizing that within a pluralistic society efforts to censor may exist, such challenges should be met calmly with proper respect for the beliefs of the challengers. Further, since attempts to censor sound and image material frequently arise out of misunderstanding of the rationale for using these formats, we shall attempt to help both user and censor to recognize the purpose and dynamics of communication in modern times regardless of the format.

The Association for Educational Communications and Technology is ready to cooperate with other persons or groups committed to resisting censorship or abridgement of free expression and free access to ideas and information.

Adopted by:
AECT Board of Directors
Kansas City
April 21, 1978

## Selected Research Studies

Compiled by Elaine K. Didier

### *Elementary Library Media Programs*

Ainsworth, Len. "An Objective Measure of the Impact of a Library Learning Center." *School Libraries* 18 (Winter 1969): 33–35.

Improved library skills through instruction in library usage and access to full-service program staffed by professionals.

Bailey, Gertrude. "The Use of a Library Resource Program for the Improvement of Language Abilities of Disadvantaged First Grade Pupils of an Urban Community." Ed.D. dissertation, Boston College, 1970.

Participation in an active library media program improved overall language ability and verbal expression.

Becker, Dale Eugene. "Social Studies Achievement of Pupils in Schools with Libraries and Schools without Libraries." Ed.D. dissertation, University of Pennsylvania, 1970.

Access to a library and the presence of a librarian enhanced achievement in information-gathering skills and reading of charts and graphs.

DeBlauw, Robert Allen. "Effect of a Multi-Media Program on Achievement and Attitudes of Elementary and Secondary Students." Ph.D. dissertation, Iowa State University, 1973.

Significant gains in achievement in vocabulary, word study skills, and arithmetic.

Didier, Elaine K. Macklin. "Relationships between Student Achievement in Reading and Library Media Programs and Personnel." Ph.D. dissertation, University of Michigan, 1982.

Significant improvement in reading scores, study skills, and access to the library in schools with library media programs staffed by full-time professionals.

Gaver, Mary Virginia. *Effectiveness of Centralized Library Service in Elementary Schools,* 2nd ed. New Brunswick, N.J.; Rutgers University Press, 1963.

Higher educational gains in reading and library skills in schools with libraries staffed by qualified librarians.

Gengler, Charles Richard. "A Study of Selected Problem Solving Skills Comparing Teacher Instructed Students with Librarian-Teacher Instructed Students." Ed.D. dissertation, University of Oregon, 1965.

Significant increase in ability to solve problems and locate, organize, and evaluate information through instruction by librarians as well as teachers.

Harmer, William R. "The Effect of a Library Training Program on Summer Loss or Gain in Reading Abilities." Ph.D. dissertation, University of Minnesota, 1959.

Instruction in library use increased amount of reading and overall reading ability.

Loertscher, David V., May Lein Ho, and Melvin M. Bowie. "Exemplary Elementary Schools and Their Library Media Centers: A Research Report." *School Library Media Quarterly* (Spring, 1987): 147–153.

Reviews services, staffing and collections of exemplary programs, and identified the threshold of a full-service media program as requiring a full-time professional and a full-time clerical worker.

Masterton, Elizabeth. "An Evaluation of the School Library in the Reading Program of the School." M.A. dissertation, University of Chicago, 1963.

Higher reading scores were reported for students who attended schools that had centralized libraries staffed by professional librarians.

McMillen, Ralph Donnelley. "An Analysis of Library Programs and a Determination of the Educational Justification of These Programs in Selected Elementary Schools of Ohio." Ed.D. dissertation, Western Reserve University, 1965.

Superior reading comprehension, knowledge and use of reference materials were found in students in schools with full-time librarians.

Monahan, Marietta. "A Comparison of Student Reading in Elementary Schools with and without a Central Library." M.A. dissertation, University of Chicago, 1956.

Students with access to a centralized library read more books of high quality and greater variety than did those without.

Wilson, Ella Jean. "Evaluating Urban Centralized Elementary School Libraries." Ph.D. dissertation, Wayne State University, 1965.

Higher standardized test scores, particularly in the areas of reading ability and library skills, were found in schools with libraries staffed by professionals.

Yarling, James Robert. "Children's Understandings and Use of Selected Library-Related Skills in Two Elementary Schools, One with and One without a Centralized Library." Ed.D. dissertation, Ball State University, 1968.

Students in the school with a centralized library had significantly improved outlining and note-taking skills, verbal expression and general library skills.

## Secondary Library Media Programs

Barrilleaux, Louis E. "An Experimental Investigation of the Effects of Multiple Library Sources as Compared to the Use of a Basic Textbook on Student Achievement and Learning Activity in Junior High Science." Ph.D. dissertation, University of Iowa, 1965.

Intensive use of library resources for science instruction resulted in significant improvement in critical thinking, science attitudes, writing, elective science reading, and overall library utilization.

Greve, Clyde LeRoy. "The Relationship of the Availability of Libraries to Academic Achievement of High School Seniors." Ph.D. dissertation, University of Denver, 1974.

A direct, positive correlation was found between academic achievement (Iowa Tests of Educational Development) and the level of library services available.

Hale, Irene W. "October Inspiration: School Libraries Work!" *Wilson Library Bulletin* 45 (October 1970): 127.

Overall improvement in academic achievement (Scholastic Aptitude Test, verbal) resulted from intensive library instruction and access to a full-service media program.

Hastings, Dorothy, and Daniel Tanner. "The Influence of Library Work in Improving English Language Skills at the High School Level." *Journal of Experimental Education* 31 (Summer 1963): 401–405.

Higher scores in spelling and total language skills were realized through regular use of the library.

McConnaha, Virginia. "The Effect of an Elementary School Library at High School Level." *California School Libraries* 43 (Summer 1972): 24–29.

Increased knowledge of library skills were found in junior high students who attended elementary schools where librarians provided library instruction.

Thorne, Lucile M. "The Influence of the Knapp School Libraries Project on the Reading Comprehension and on the Knowledge of Library Skills of the Pupils at the Farrar Junior High School, Provo, Utah." Ed.D. dissertation, Brigham Young University, 1967.

Significant gains in reading comprehension and library skills were made by students who had access to a full service library media program.

## Post-Secondary Education

Harkin, Willard Dwight. "Analysis of Secondary School Library Media Programs in Relation to Academic Success of Ball State University Students in Their Freshman and Sophomore Years." Ph.D. dissertation, Ball State University, 1971.

No significant difference was found in academic achievement among students from schools with high or low ratios of media to students.

Snider, Felix Eugene. "The Relationship of Library Ability to Performance in College." Ph.D. dissertation, University of Illinois, 1965.

A strong positive correlation was found between library skills and academic achievement (GPA).

Walker, Richard Dean. "The Influence of Antecedent Library Service Upon Academic Achievement of University of Illinois Freshman." Ph.D. dissertation, University of Illinois, 1963.

No significant difference was determined in achievement (GPA) among students from schools with high or low levels of school and public library service available.

## Education of Library Media Personnel

Gaver, Mary Virginia. *Patterns of Development in Elementary School Libraries Today: A Five Year Report on Emerging Media Centers.* 3rd ed. Chicago: Britannica, 1969.

School libraries staffed by professional librarians were found to provide a greater variety and number of activities and services than those without.

Hodowanec, George V. "Comparison of Academic Training with Selected Job Responsibilities of Media Specialists." Ed.D. dissertation, Temple University, 1973.

Loertscher, David V., and Phyllis Land. "An Empirical Study of Media Services in Indiana Elementary Schools." *School Media Quarterly* 4 (Fall 1975): 8–18.

Full-time media specialists provide a significantly greater number of library services than do part-time professionals or full-time clerical staff.

Natarella, Margaret Dietrich. "A Survey of Media Center Personnel and School Policies that Relate to Students and Trade Books in Selected

Michigan Elementary Schools." Ph.D. dissertation, Michigan State University, 1972.

Media programs staffed by degreed personnel (with or without certification) provide a significantly greater number of activities and services than those staffed by non-degreed personnel.

Wert, Lucille M. *Library Education and High School Library Services*. Washington D.C.: U.S. Department of Health, Education and Welfare, Office of Education, 1969.

Librarians with graduate education (master's degree) offer more extensive services and their libraries are more heavily used than those with lesser-educated staff.

## Curricular Role of the Library Media Specialist

Blazek, Ron. *Influencing Students toward Media Center Use: An Experimental Investigation in Mathematics*. Chicago: American Library Association, 1975.

Significant increase in usage of mathematics and other library materials as a result of teacher example and referral.

Ducat, O.P., Sister Mary Peter Claver. "Student and Faculty Use of the Library in Three Secondary Schools." D.L.S. dissertation, Columbia University, 1960.

Role of the library in the educational program of the school is strongly affected by the importance teachers ascribe to materials in achieving their teaching objectives.

Griffin, Edith McClenny. "Library Instructional Support Services in Elementary Schools in the District of Columbia Public School System." Ed.D. dissertation, American University, 1980.

Age, education, and familiarity with media are major factors affecting teachers' utilization of library media services. Teachers with education in library science or audio-visual media are more likely to utilize sophisticated media services and work closely with the media specialist.

Hodges, Gerald C. "The Instructional Role of the School Library Media Specialist: What Research Says to Us." *School Library Media Quarterly* 9 (Summer 1981): 281–285.

Identifies factors affecting the curricular role of the media specialist, including size of media staff, competencies in curriculum planning, materials evaluations, and instructional design.

Hsu, Oon Bee. "The Image of the School Library as Reflected in the Opinions and Student Use of the Library in Selected Secondary Schools." Ed.S. dissertation, University of Michigan, 1970.

Contribution of the library to the total educational program is conditioned by teachers' usage and view of its importance.

Johnson, Harlan. "Teacher Utilization of Librarians in the Secondary Schools of Tucson District No. 1." Ed.D. dissertation, University of Arizona, 1975.

Teachers have very traditional expectations of librarians and do not seek their involvement in curriculum design or instructional development.

Mohajerin, Kathryn S., and Earl P. Smith. "Perceptions of the Role of the School Media Specialist." *School Media Quarterly* 9 (Spring 1981): 153–163.

Demonstrates significant differences in perception of the role of library media specialists between media educators and principals, teachers and practicing media specialists, with the former having higher performance expectations.

Newman, Joan A., Richard D. Klausmeier, and John Bullard. "Iowa Survey Shows: Teachers Need More Training in Media." Iowa City: University of Iowa, 1974. ERIC Document 105895.

Teachers' and principals' failure to utilize instructional media and library services stems from lack of training in the areas of equipment use and selection of media, as well as lack of awareness of the media specialist's function.

Rogers, JoAnn Vedder. "Teachers and Media Resources in Selected Appalachian Secondary Schools: A Study of Attitudes, Usage and Knowledge of Media Center Fundamentals." Ph.D. dissertation, University of Pittsburgh, 1977.

Teachers' use of media is directly related to their attitude toward and competency with media.

Stroud, Janet Gossard. "Evaluation of Media Center Services by Media Staff, Teachers and Students in Indiana Middle and Junior High Schools." Ph.D. dissertation, Purdue University, 1976.

Teachers' use of the library media center is influenced by sex, years of experience, and subject area taught; media specialists' experience contributes to the range and number of services offered; only one-third of media specialists take an active role in instructional planning.

Turner, Philip M. "Research on Helping Teachers Teach." In "Current Research" column edited by Jacqueline C. Mancall. *School Library Media Quarterly* 15 (Summer 1987): 229–231.

Reviews factors contributing to media specialists' role in instructional design.

# Contributors

## AASL/AECT Standards Writing Committee

Chairperson: James W. Liesener*
Professor, College of Library & Information Services
University of Maryland
College Park, Maryland

Ruth V. Bell*
Director of Library Media Services
Blue Valley Unified School District 229
Stanley, Kansas

Diane deCordova Biesel
Library Media Specialist
River Edge Elementary School
Dumont, New Jersey

Rebecca T. Bingham
Director of Library Media Services
Jefferson County Public Schools
Louisville, Kentucky

Carolyn Cain*
Director of Library Media Services
LaFollette High School
Madison, Wisconsin

Judith F. Davie
Director of School Media Programs
Greensboro Public Schools
Greensboro, North Carolina

Bernard Franckowiak
Director of Libraries
University of Lowell
Lowell, Massachusetts

Robert G. Hale
Connecticut State Department of Education
Learning & Resources Technology
Hartford, Connecticut

Winona Jones
Library Media Specialist
East Lake High School
Tarpon Springs, Florida

Addie P. Kinsinger*
KAET-TV ASSET
Arizona State University
Tempe, Arizona

Jane Love
Library Media Specialist
Old Mill Senior High School
Glen Burnie, Maryland

* Denotes members of the AASL/AECT Standards Writing Team

Jeanette M. Smith
Director of Media Services
Forsyth Country Day School
Lewisville, North Carolina

Project Assistant:
Susan Myers
University of Maryland
College Park, Maryland

## Consultants

Shirley L. Aaron
Professor, Florida State University
Tallahassee, Florida

Lucy E. Ainsley
Director, Instructional
  Technology
Birmingham Public Schools
Birmingham, Michigan

David Barnard
Dean, Learning Resources
University of Wisconsin–Stout
Menomonie, Wisconsin

Daniel D. Barron
Associate Professor
University of South Carolina
Columbia, South Carolina

James Bennett
Library Media Specialist
Shoreham-Wading River Senior
  High School
Shoreham, New York

Rolland G. Billings
Director, Media Services
Ann Arbor Public Schools
Ann Arbor, Michigan

Elsie L. Brumback
Assistant State Superintendent
Media & Technology Services
Raleigh, North Carolina

Margaret Chisholm
Director, Graduate School of
  Library & Information Science
University of Washington
Seattle, Washington

J. Gordon Coleman, Jr.
Assistant Professor
Graduate School of Library
  Service
University of Alabama
University, Alabama

Jeannine Cronkhite
Resource Dissemination
  Specialist
Wayne County Intermediate
  School District
Wayne, Michigan

Donald P. Ely
Director, ERIC Clearinghouse
  on Learning Resources
Syracuse, New York

Linda F. Erz
LFE Design
Eugene, Oregon

Shirley A. Fitzgibbons
Associate Professor
School of Library & Information
  Science
Indiana University
Bloomington, Indiana

Richard Gilkey
Director, Educational Media
Portland Public Schools
Portland, Oregon

David L. Graf
Program Director
University of Wisconsin–Stout
Menomonie, Wisconsin

Margaret Hayes Grazier
Detroit, Michigan

Karen Harris
Professor, Library Science
University of New Orleans
New Orleans, Louisiana

Harry Herbert
Assistant Dean for Learning
    Resources
University of Wisconsin-Stout
Menomonie, Wisconsin

Dianne McAfee Hopkins
Assistant Professor
School of Library & Information
    Studies
University of Wisconsin-Madison
Madison, Wisconsin

William E. Hug
Department of Educational
    Media & Librarianship
University of Georgia
Athens, Georgia

Milbrey L. Jones
U.S. Department of Education
Washington, D.C.

Eleanor R. Kulleseid
Director, Learning Resources
    Center
Bank Street College of Education
New York, New York

Bernice Lamkin
Director of Media Services/Staff
    Development
Forest Hills Public Schools
Grand Rapids, Michigan

David V. Loertscher
Senior Acquisition Editor
Libraries Unlimited
Littleton, Colorado

Jacqueline C. Mancall
Associate Professor
College of Information Studies
Drexel University
Philadelphia, Pennsylvania

Carolyn Markuson
Supervisor of Library &
    Instructional Materials
Brookline Schools
Brookline, Massachusetts

Patricia H. Mautino
Director of Instructional Support
    & Information Services
Oswego County Board of
    Cooperative Educational
    Services
Mexico, New York

Frances M. McDonald
Associate Professor
Library Media Education
    Department
Mankato State University
Mankato, Minnesota

Marilyn L. Miller
Chairperson
Library Science/Educational
    Technology Department
University of North
    Carolina-Greensboro
Greensboro, North Carolina

Retta Patrick
Consultant
Little Rock, Arkansas

Fred C. Pfister
Professor, School of Library &
    Information Science
University of South Florida
Tampa, Florida

Patricia B. Pond
Beaverton, Oregon

Emanuel Prostano
Dean, School of Library Science
   & Instructional Technology
Southern Connecticut State
   University
New Haven, Connecticut

Felix C. Robb
Executive Director Emeritus
Southern Association of Colleges
   & Schools
Atlanta, Georgia

Isabel Schon
Professor, Reading Education &
   Library Science
Arizona State University
Tempe, Arizona

Anthony C. Schulzetenberg
Consultant
St. Cloud, Minnesota

Richard J. Sorensen
School Library Media Supervisor
Wisconsin Department of Public
   Instruction
Madison, Wisconsin

Roger N. Tipling
Associate Professor
College of Education
Southwest Missouri State
   University
Springfield, Missouri

Philip M. Turner
Professor, Graduate School of
   Library Service
University of Alabama
University, Alabama

Phyllis Van Orden
Professor, School of Library &
   Information Studies
Florida State University
Tallahassee, Florida

Kay E. Vandergrift
Assistant Professor
School of Communications,
   Information & Library Studies
Rutgers University
New Brunswick, New Jersey

Howard D. White
Associate Professor
College of Information Studies
Drexel University
Philadelphia, Pennsylvania

Ralph L. Whiting
Director, Library
   Media Services
LaCrosse School District
LaCrosse, Wisconsin

## Executive Editorial Committee

Elaine K. Didier
Director, Kresge Business
   Administration Library
University of Michigan
Ann Arbor, Michigan

Ann Carlson Weeks
Executive Director
American Association of
   School Librarians
American Library Association
Chicago, Illinois

Karen A. Whitney
Library Director
Agua Fria Union High School
Avondale, Arizona

Stanley Zenor
Executive Director
Association for Educational
   Communications and Tech-
   nology
Washington, D.C.

## AASL 1987–1988 Board of Directors

President: Karen Whitney
Library Director
Agua Fria Union High School
Avondale, Arizona

Vice-president: Jacqueline G.
  Morris
Indiana Department of Education
Indianapolis, Indiana

Past president: Marilyn L. Miller
Chair, Library Science/
  Educational Technology
  Department
University of North Carolina
Greensboro, North Carolina

Secretary: Delores Z. Pretlow
Supervisor of Media Services
Richmond Public Schools
Richmond, Virginia

Roger Ashley
Library Media Center Director
Andover High School
Bloomfield, Michigan

Frank R. Birmingham
Chair, Library Media Education
  Department
Mankato State University
Mankato, Minnesota

Constance J. Champlin
Multimedia Services Director
Washington Township
Indianapolis, Indiana

Anne Masters
Director, Media Services
Norman Public Schools
Norman, Oklahoma

Nancy Minnich
Library Director
Tower Hill School Library
Wilmington, Delaware

Karen K. Niemeyer
Director, Media Services
Carmel Clay Schools
Carmel, Indiana

Pamela Parman
Library Media Specialist
Maryville High School
Maryville, Tennessee

Retta Patrick
Consultant
Little Rock, Arkansas

Beverley C. Rentschler
Consolidated Schools
Walled Lake, Michigan

Merrilyn Ridgeway
Arizona Department of
  Education
Phoenix, Arizona

M. Maggie Rogers
Northwest Regional Education
  Laboratory
Portland, Oregon

Helen Lloyd Snoke
Professor, School of Library
  Science
University of Michigan
Ann Arbor, Michigan

Sue Albertson Walker
Director, Curriculum
School District of Lancaster
Lancaster, Pennsylvania

Charles White
Consultant, State Department of
  Education
Hartford, Connecticut

## AECT 1987–1988 Board of Directors

President: Elaine K. Didier
Director, Kresge Business
   Administration Library
University of Michigan
Ann Arbor, Michigan

Vice-president: Don Smellie
Head, Instructional Technology
   Department
Utah State University
Logan, Utah

Past president: Robert G. Hale
Coordinator, Learning Resources
   & Technologies Unit
State Department of Education
Hartford, Connecticut

Secretary-Treasurer: Roger N.
   Tipling
Associate Professor
College of Education
Southwest Missouri State
   University
Springfield, Missouri

Charles G. Forsythe
Director, Instructional Materials
   Center
Montgomery County
Erdenheim, Pennsylvania

David L. Graf
Program Director
Media Technology Graduate
   Program
University of Wisconsin–Stout
Menomonie, Wisconsin

Barbara Hakes
Head, Educational Foundations
   & Instructional Technology
College of Education
University of Wyoming
Laramie, Wyoming

Stanley A. Huffman, Jr.
Director, Distance Learning
Virginia Tech University
Blacksburg, Virginia

Addie P. Kinsinger
Consultant, KAET-TV ASSET
Arizona State University
Tempe, Arizona

David L. Little
President, RMI Media
   Productions
Shawnee Mission, Kansas

Robert R. Ruezinsky
Director, Media & Technology
Montclair State College
Upper Montclair, New Jersey

Ralph Whiting
Director, Library Media Services
LaCrosse School District
LaCrosse, Wisconsin

# Financial Contributors

## Honor Roll*

American Association of School Librarians, Alaska

Arizona State Library Association, School Libraries Division

J. Gordon Coleman, Jr.

Educational Media Association of New Jersey

Florida Association for Media in Education

Thomas L. Hart

Iowa Educational Media Association

Leon County (Fla.) Media Specialists

Michigan Association for Media in Education

Missouri Association of School Librarians

North Carolina Association of School Librarians

Oklahoma Association for Educational Communications and Technology

Paul W. Welliver

* Contributions of $100 or more from individuals and of $1 per member or $500 or more from associations.

## Sustaining Contributors*

Arizona Educational Media
Association

California Media and Library
Educators Association

Hawaii Association of School
Librarians

Illinois Association for Media in
Education

Nebraska Educational Media
Association

New York Library Association,
School Library Media Section

South Carolina Association of
School Librarians

## Contributors**

Arkansas Audio Visual
Association

Association for Indiana Media
Educators

Dorothy W. Blake

Colorado Educational Media
Association

Connecticut Educational Media
Association

Lavinia M. Connors

Clara G. Hoover

Ethelene D. Jones

Kentucky School Media
Association

Maine Educational Media
Association

Maryland Educational Media
Organization

Stephen L. Matthews

Minnesota Educational Media
Organization

National Association of State
Educational Media
Professionals

Nebraska Library Association,
School, Children's and Young
People's Section

Ohio Educational Library Media
Association

Oregon Educational Media
Association, Inc.

Pennsylvania School Library
Association, Inc.

Rhode Island Media Association

Kathleen A. Smith

Pat Thurman

University of Texas at Austin,
GSLIS

Virginia Library Association

Wisconsin Educational Media
Association

* Contributions of $50 or more from individuals and of $.50 per member or $250 or more from associations.

** Contributions of $25 or more from individuals and of $.25 per member or $100 or more from associations.

# Bibliography

Prepared by David V. Loertscher

## History of School Libraries

Bowie, Melvin, comp. *Historic Documents of School Libraries*. Fayetteville, Ark.: Hi Willow, 1976.

Collected in photoreproduction form are a number of important early documents of school libraries, including the 1877 history of school libraries, the C. C. Certain standards, and the Cecil and Heaps history of school libraries.

Branyan, Brenda M. *Outstanding Women Who Promoted the Concept of the Unified School Library and Audiovisual Programs, 1950 through 1975*. Fayetteville, Ark.: Hi Willow, 1981.

The accomplishments of the early pioneers of school libraries. Concentrates on: Eleanor Ahlers, Elenora Alexander, Cora Paul Bomar, Esther Burrin, Leila Ann Doyle, Ruth Ersted, Sara Fenwick, Mildred Frary, Mary V. Gaver, Frances Hatfield, Sue Hefley, Frances Henne, Phyllis Hochstettler, Mary Frances Johnson, Mildred Krohn, Helen Lloyd, Alice Lohrer, Jean Lowrie, Mary Helen Mahar, Alice Brooks McGuire, Virginia McJenkin, Marie McMahan, Marilyn Miller, Margaret Nicholsen, Mildred Nickel, LuOuida Phillips, Elnora Portteus, Lillian Shapiro, Sara Srygley, Peggy Sullivan, Mary Ann Swanson, Lorraine Tolman, Carolyn Whitenack, and Elinor Yungmeyer.

Gillespie, John T., and Diana L. Spirt. *Creating a School Media Program*. New York: R. R. Bowker, 1973.

Chapter 1 includes a brief history of the school library media center.

Greenman, Edward D. "The Development of Secondary School Libraries." *Library Journal* 38 (April 1913): 184.

Hall, Mary E. "The Development of the Modern High School Library." *Library Journal* 40 (September 1915): 627.

Lembo, Diana L. (Spirt). *A History of the Growth and Development of the Department of Audiovisual Instruction of the NEA from 1923 to 1968*. Ph.D. dissertation, New York University, 1970.

_____and Carol Bruce. "The Growth and Development of the Depart-

ment of Audiovisual Instruction: 1923–1968." *Audiovisual Instruction* (in 10 parts, v. 16, September 1971, through v. 17, June/July 1972).
A summary of Diana Lembo's dissertation.

Pond, Patricia Brown. "The American Association of School Librarians: The Origins and Development of a National Professional Association for School Librarians, 1895–1951." Ph.D. dissertation, University of Chicago, 1982.

_____."Development of a Professional School Library Association: American Association of School Librarians." *School Media Quarterly* 5 (Fall 1976): 12–18.
A summary of the author's dissertation.

_____."The History of AASL: Origins and Development, 1896–1951." In Shirley L. Aaron and Pat R. Scales, *School Library Media Annual* 1: 113–131 (Littleton, Colo.: Libraries Unlimited, 1983).
A summary of the author's dissertation.

_____."Seeking Recognition for Early Leaders in School Library Service." *Interchange* 16, no. 2 (Winter 1987): 18–21.
Interesting character sketches of early school library pioneers, including Martha Wilson, Harriet Wood, Martha Pritchard, Lucile Fargo, and Mary Hall.

Spirt, Diana L. "Best Wishes for the Next Fifty: A Brief Overview of the AECT from 1923 to 1973." *LJ/SLJ Previews* 1 (April 1973): 5–10.
A summary of the Diana Lembo dissertation listed above.

### Editions of National Standards and Guidelines for School Library Media Programs

Certain, C. C. "Standard Library Organization and Equipment for Secondary Schools of Different Sizes." National Education Association, Department of Secondary Education, 1920.

_____."Elementary School Library Standards." Prepared under the supervision of a Joint Committee of the National Education Association and the American Library Association. Chicago: American Library Association, 1925.

Committees on Post-War Planning of the American Library Association. *School Libraries for Today and Tomorrow, Functions and Standards*. Chicago: American Library Association, 1945.

American Association of School Librarians. *Standards for School Library Programs*. Chicago: American Library Association, 1960.

_____and the Department of Audiovisual Instruction of the National Education Association. *Standards for School Media Programs*. Chicago: American Library Association, 1969.

_____and Association for Educational Communications and Technology. *Media Programs District and School*. Chicago: American Library Association, 1975.

# Index

Prepared by Pamela Hori

Cover Design by Kathy Braun
Text Design by Marcie Lange

Composed by Point West
   in Stymie
   on a Quadex typesetting
   system

Printed on 50-pound Glatfelter,
   a pH-neutral stock, and bound
   in 10-point Carolina cover stock
   by Port City, Inc.
   ∞

Photo Credits
   Birmingham (Mich.) Public Schools
   Wichita (Kan.) Public Schools
   Richmond (Va.) Public Schools